*L*ONGRIDGE
THE WAY WE WERE

Compiled by Longridge and
District Local History Society
to celebrate the Millennium

Edited by
Mike Pattinson

LONGRIDGE
THE WAY WE WERE

Compiled by Longridge and District
Local History Society to celebrate the Millennium

Edited by
Mike Pattinson

ISBN 0-9533643-4-8

Published by
Hudson History
of Settle.

Designed and typeset by Phil Hudson of Hudson History, Procter House,
Kirkgate, Settle. BD24 9DZ.

CONTENTS

Cover photograph "Longridge Peace Procession, 1919"

ACKNOWLEDGMENTS

As Editor, I should like to record my thanks to all the people who contributed to the making of this book. Like all historians, the writers of the articles are particularly indebted to archivists and librarians. We are grateful for the help given by the staffs of the Lancashire Record Office; Longridge Library; Lancashire Local Studies Library; Harris Reference Library and Harris Museum and Art Gallery, Preston; and the Co-operative Union Archive, Manchester; especially David Shuttleworth, Louise Connell and Gillian Lonergan. The Lancashire Evening Post Ltd. and the Guild Community Healthcare NHS Trust kindly gave permission to reproduce material and illustrations in their copyright or ownership. Gillian Whalley and Mavis Wilkinson of the Longridge News have assisted with information and publicity. Individuals who made valuable contributions were Alan Crosby with sound advice, Joe Howson with help at Lee House and Barrie Marshall and John Britnell with photographic expertise. Longridge Local History Society allowed us to reproduce photographs from its collection, many donated by the people of Longridge and district, and both committee and members supported this project. Tom Heginbotham, Brian Bamber and Ken Willan lent their own material.

Generous financial assistance was provided by Ribble Valley Borough Council and Longridge Town Council, through the good offices of John Baldwin and Martin Taylor. Our publisher, Phil Hudson of Hudson History of Settle, has been very helpful at all stages in transforming the idea and the manuscript into the final format with a speed not always associated with the book trade.

I wish to express my warmest thanks to all the contributors for their co-operation and good humour, in the hope that this book meets with their approval, and also to my wife, Penelope, for her patience, support and assistance with the new technology.

FOREWORD BY THE MAYOR OF RIBBLE VALLEY

I greatly appreciate being asked to write a Foreword to this fascinating work. As Mayor in the millennium year, I am especially conscious of the need to re-evaluate our past, to understand our evolving social fabric and to seek fresh insights into our communities.

This is an excellent attempt to place on record many aspects of the history of the Longridge area. I recognise the amount of work that has gone into collecting information and photographs, and the contributors' enthusiasm for their research shines through. Their articles will bring back memories to many readers, and I hope will inspire others to take a keener interest in local history.

I am delighted at this initiative by Longridge Local History Society and commend it as an entertaining and informative read to everybody who cares about our past.

> Coun. Brian Collis
> Mayor of Ribble Valley

FOREWORD BY THE TOWN MAYOR OF LONGRIDGE

I was very pleased to be asked to contribute a Foreword to this new publication on aspects of the history of Longridge and district. At a time of rapid change, when we have just witnessed a total eclipse and are about to celebrate the millennium, a project that contributes materially to our understanding of the past is particularly welcome.

For over 20 years, the Longridge Local History Society has helped to focus attention on our heritage, through its ambitious programme of talks and visits. We are fortunate that local history attracts such dedicated enthusiasts. The authors of these articles are to be congratulated on their considerable research and thanked for their efforts in recording bygone events for our descendants. They have produced an interesting book and I wish it every success.

> Coun. Pam Cliff
> Town Mayor of Longridge

ABOUT THE CONTRIBUTORS

MIKE KEENEY
Mike and his family have lived in Longridge since 1986. In recent years he and other members of the Longridge and District Local History Society have been researching Longridge and its past. His other interests include British political history, the railways of Britain, cricket and bridge.

RONALD SEED
A native of Longridge, Ron attended R. Smith's Boys School and Balshaws Grammar School. Joined Longridge Industrial Co-operative Society in 1940 and also served in the RAF Volunteer Reserve as a Wireless Operator. Secretary and General Manager of the Society 1970-1981. After retirement was Chairman of Brockhall Hospital, Clerk to Longridge Town Council and Secretary of Longridge British Legion.

LEO WARREN
Born in Accrington and educated at St. Mary's College, Blackburn and the University of London. Has taught history at Preston Catholic College and subsequently Cardinal Newman College for 39 years. Has a long-standing interest in the Catholic history of Lancashire.

PETER VICKERS
Born in 1938 at Lostock Hall with grandparents from Chipping and Whitechapel. Educated at Balshaws Grammar School and much later at Lancashire Polytechnic where he studied Geography and American Studies, then social history for his MA. Widowed, with three grown-up children, he spends his time organising and playing jazz music and researching social history, especially popular pastimes.

JOHN EARNSHAW

Moved to Longridge 20 years ago. In 1995 suggested that it would be appropriate to make a permanent record of the effects of the war on the people of Longridge to mark the 50th. anniversary of the end of the war. Currently Chairman of Longridge and District Local History Society and as such suggested the Society should produce a further volume on the history of Longridge to commemorate the Millennium.

HAROLD IDDON

Worked for many years as an administrator at Whittingham Hospital and was responsible for producing its centenary history on behalf of the Hospital Management Committee.

ALAN DODD

Born in Birkenhead in 1929. After an apprenticeship in the building trade and study at the Liverpool College of Building, served in the Far East on National Service and worked for the Mersey Docks and Harbour Board, the Atomic Energy Authority and Hawker Siddeley Aviation. Later Group Building Supervisor at Whittingham Hospital. Married with one daughter, and lives in Goosnargh.

MIKE PATTINSON

Born in Longridge in 1944. Educated at Clitheroe Royal Grammar School, Leeds University and Leeds Polytechnic. Worked in public libraries in Lancashire and Cheshire and as Librarian at the University of Humberside, before returning to Longridge as Vice-Principal at Alston Hall College. Lives in Grimsargh. Married with two children.

INTRODUCTION

The ideal millennium project should be one that enables people to understand the past better, to celebrate this moment in time and to make a contribution to the future. As well as a commemoration, it is an opportunity for reflection.

In considering how best it could mark the millennium, Longridge Local History Society felt that it would be particularly appropriate to record aspects of the history of the Longridge area in a form which would be available to both present and future generations.

In 1993, J. M. Till, who was then Chairman of the Society, published "A History of Longridge and its People", the first full-scale chronicle of the village since Tom C. Smith wrote his "History of Longridge and District in 1888". Both provide excellent records and source books for the evolution of the community. In his introductory remarks, Mr. Till stated that, *"There are, of course, many aspects of Longridge history which have not been touched, but those must await further research"*. Sadly, he died before he could undertake that research. This volume is intended to fill some of the gaps and should be of interest to local people and to incomers.

Longridge Local History Society is made up of both groups. Involvement with the Society may have been helpful in finding a way into community life, in sharing a common interest, even in dealing with life changes. It is hoped that this initiative in local history will add to the sense of coherence and integration in the locality, and contribute towards the community spirit fostered by other millennium events. The co-operative nature of this publishing venture, with articles from a number of contributors and financial support from two local councils, reflects the parts played in the development of Longridge by its pioneering building society and co-operative movement.

Although this volume will coincide with the millennium, its articles illustrate that local history is concerned with change over time, rather than a single snapshot view of the past. It is motivated by curiosity about, and attachment to, the locality where people live and "belong" - that elusive sense of place and identity composed of topography, predominant industries, customs, speech characteristics, family history and memory. In an age which recognises the value of heritage and tradition, it is ironic that we often do not appreciate what we have until we have lost it.

For example, for those born, bred and buttered in Longridge, woken in the morning by the sound of front doors slamming and the tramp of clogs to mills and factories, what was an everyday experience as recently as the 1950s has completely disappeared.

It is hoped that readers will find this book informative and entertaining, and will be encouraged to preserve material relevant to local history, to record their experiences and to carry out their own research. Please enjoy these memories of the way we were.

Mike Pattinson
Editor

THE HISTORY OF BERRY LANE IN LONGRIDGE

Mike Keeney

We must all be able to think of main streets in various towns and villages that are of some antiquity and containing buildings of different size, shape and age. Many of these places we will find attractive and enjoy revisiting. When turning to Berry Lane in Longridge, the first two categories apply regarding the buildings, but there is next to nothing above one hundred and fifty years old. Does this lead one to conclude that this thoroughfare is hardly worth describing in any detail? I believe this is not the case considering the growth and development of Berry Lane, which has seen many changes to the pattern of its life beginning in the second quarter of the nineteenth century. Changes and alterations which are continuing today.

It is not possible to tell, or even to estimate, how long a track or route has existed along what we now call Berry Lane. The 1837 tithe map of Alston and the 1838 tithe map of Dilworth show it as a road, almost empty of buildings, linking two through routes. However, the main roads in the town at that time were the two arteries of the road from Preston that divided at the Old Oak site (the building was in situ but possibly not yet an inn) and the road diverging from the top of Fell Brow leading to Goosnargh. Of these the most important was the road past St. Lawrence's church leading up to the market place and onward to Clitheroe or Chipping across the fell. The other two crossed one another at Four Lane Ends, a crossroads with its own little duckpond and now known as Stone Bridge.

Surely one would say, the derivation of the name Berry Lane is straightforward? But no, nothing so simple as it once having had trees producing berries along its route. The 1844 six inches to one mile Ordnance Survey map calls it Burey Lane with a small group of buildings known as Burey Houses on part of what was later to become a cotton mill. An 1868 advertisement in a newspaper called the *Preston Pilot* refers to it as Bury Lane, only for the Ordnance Survey map of 1892 to show the current spelling.

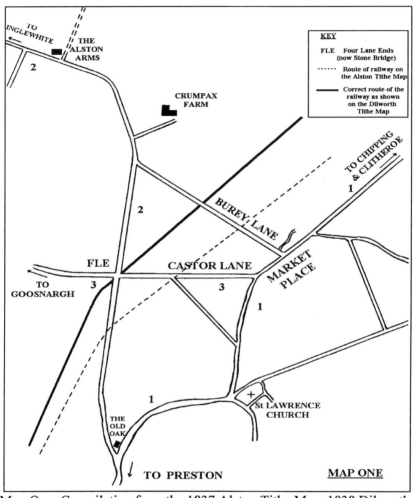

KEY

FLE Four Lane Ends
     (now Stone Bridge)

······ Route of railway on
        the Alston Tithe Map

——— Correct route of the
     railway as shown
     on the Dilworth
     Tithe Map

TO INGLEWHITE

THE ALSTON ARMS

2

CRUMPAX FARM

BUREY LANE

TO CHIPPING & CLITHEROE

1

2

FLE

CASTOR LANE

MARKET PLACE

TO GOOSNARGH

3

3

1

1

St LAWRENCE CHURCH

THE OLD OAK

TO PRESTON

MAP ONE

Map One: Compilation from the 1837 Alston Tithe Map, 1838 Dilworth
Tithe Map and the 1844 6" to 1 mile Ordnance Survey Map.
The Three Main Routes in Longridge at that Time.
1. The Old Oak, via Chapel Hill and Market Place and across the
fell to Clitheroe.
2. The Old Oak, via Four Lane Ends and the Alston Arms to
Inglewhite.
3. From Market Place via Castor Lane (Kestor Lane) and Four
Lane Ends to Goosnargh.

Regarding the earliest spelling as Burey, this is not in the *Oxford English Dictionary* (Second Edition) as an earlier version of the word bury. A property on what is now Inglewhite Road was called Burey on the tithe map later becoming Berry House. Like the origin of the Jeffrey in Jeffrey Hill, Burey remains unsolved. Bury has a little more rationale about it, but where was there a burial place? One possible suggestion is that at some stage there was a settlement near Longridge. The "worth" of Dilworth means enclosure which if big enough could have had a burial area. However, to date that remains only a theory as no site has been found. Whether the change from Bury to Berry was a deliberate decision or just gradually altered is uncertain, as is the change from Castor to Kestor Lane.

When the Dilworth tithe map surveyor stood surveying the scene at the top of what is now Berry Lane he might have been tempted to wonder why the name did not continue right up to the road junction. For then, as now, the last few yards were part of Market Place. The surveyor's view would have been one of fields and hedges on either side of the slope and into the far distance. The only buildings, apart from Burey Houses mentioned earlier, were what is now number one to his left, the last in a group of buildings with the rest on Market Place and cottages on the road now called Dixon Road leading to Sharley Fold Farm, which were on his right. The nearest buildings he would see were those at Crumpax Farm set back from the lower end of the lane, but this property, dating back to 1596, was reached from what is presently Inglewhite Road.

The fields adjoining Burey Lane were mostly of several acres, owned in the main by three landowners. Thomas Dixon owned the top fields on the right, Agnes Parkinson, the lower two on that side, and The Parochial Chapel of St. Lawrence owned all the fields on the opposite side except the top one. A reference to the diagram gives full details of ownership. Looking ahead fifty years to the opening of St. Paul's Church, one is bound to ask why it was not built on the land the parish had owned. The reason will follow later, but we could quite easily have had three churches in a line on our main street.

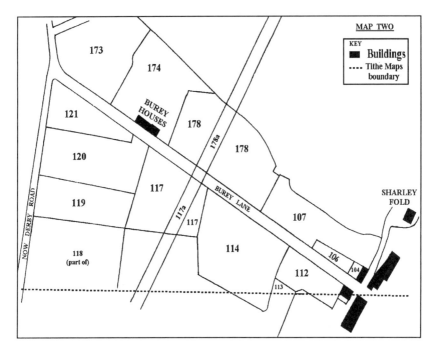

Map Two: The Ownership of Fields from the Dilworth
Tithe Map

No.   Name   Owner
112   Little Croft   Richard Strickland
113   Botch Collock. Later owned by the Sanderson family, site
         of the Slaughterhouse.
114   Great Field   Longridge Chapel
117   Great Meadow   "   "
120   Ormond Croft   "   "
121   Three Nook Croft   "   "
119, 118 and other fields adjacent to what is now Derby Road as
         far as Stone Bridge, the property of Longridge Chapel.*
104, 106 Gardens Richard Strickland
107   New Meadow Thomas Dixon of Sharley Fold
178   Lower New Field   "   "
174   Parson Meadow   Agnes Parkinson
173   Great Meadow   "   "
117A, 178A Land for Preston and Longridge Railway
Note: 117 and 173 have the same name.

* St. Lawrence's Church was still a Chapel of Ease in Ribchester Parish.

When inspecting the tithe maps we can see that our surveyor already knew that a major change was under way. The Preston and Longridge Railway company was in the process of building its line and the tithe maps include its route. The 1837 Alston map shows a different alignment with the line crossing Kestor Lane at the junction with Little Lane, then proceeding straight ahead to cross Berry Lane approximately where the Conservative Club stands today. However, the 1838 Dilworth map shows the route as built with parcel numbers allocated to the strips of land forming the route. The railway was planned and built to carry stone from the newly opened quarry owned by Thomas Fleming down to Preston. From there it could go by sea, canal or other rail routes to many destinations. Unlike many other railway projects at the time, this was the only purpose envisaged when the company was formed. It duly opened on 1st May, 1840 and, aware of the steep drop along the route, it utilised the forces of gravity to propel trucks most of the way to the terminus in Deepdale. Horses travelled down on trucks of their own to cover the last stretch, usually from about Gamull, then to return the empty wagons to the quarry. The 1844 Ordnance Survey map shows nothing more than a small hut where the line crosses Berry Lane. This would suggest a shelter for a man posted there to warn road users of impending rail traffic. It had taken the railway company five years to build its line from the convening of the first meeting to discuss the proposal. Certainly by the time of opening some return from passenger carriage had been anticipated.

Newspapers of 1840/1 record Whitsun trips to take Preston ramblers into the hills. The same source also mentions a Saturday morning horse bus from Chipping to Longridge so that its passengers could travel on a train to Preston. No special carriage was provided, transport being in stone trucks.

The Preston and Longridge Railway struggled financially from the outset and was happy to become part of an ambitious scheme to link Fleetwood with the industrial areas of Yorkshire. Full details of this and a similar plan around the time of the first world war are given in the books by Norman Parker and Joe Till listed in the bibliography. Suffice to say that in 1848 a regular passenger service was introduced using a steam locomotive, from which stage the stone traffic also was taken by the locomotive. Initially the passenger facilities were very basic, little more than a short platform, until 1872 when a station with full passenger facilities was opened on the opposite side of the track in, the building still existing today. No longer just a mineral line carrying quarried stone, the railway opened a goods yard on the opposite side of Berry Lane to the station. This led to the next big development along our road.

The cotton mills arrived fairly late in Longridge. Places like Knowle Green, with a fast flowing stream, were early on the scene utilising water power. That village once had seven in operation, with others at places such as Chipping. Longridge had just one, on the outskirts and called Spade Mill, hence the name of the reservoirs that were built there at a later date. However, by the time the railway was offering transport of a wide variety of goods traffic, steam power for mill operation was being rapidly developed. In 1850 George Whittle had opened a mill at Stone Bridge with access to the railway. In the following year Messrs William Marsden and James Hayhurst built a large spinning and weaving mill adjacent to the railway yard on field 174 (see diagram) demolishing Burey cottages in the process. Later photographs of this mill show a large three storeyed building, basically rectangular in shape and with a square chimney. The mill had a private siding linking it to the railway goods yard and running between the front of the mill and the mill workers houses on Berry Lane (now numbers 48-62). The main lodge (reservoir) was close to the road positioned where the petrol station stands today. The 1892 map shows another lodge on the side of the mill facing the railway yard, screened by a line of fir trees. The original entrance to the site was where house number 54 is now; the archway can still be seen in the stonework of that property. This was replaced by a larger entrance opposite where Arnold Swift and Sons Ltd's ironmongery and hardware premises are today. A large stone wall was built along the front of the mill and main lodge.

A visitor to the town round about 1855 would have found a village beginning to grow rapidly. Further quarries were being opened for the Longridge stone which was of high quality. Two cotton mills were providing plenty of jobs, leading to a demand for housing. A possible development which did not in the end materialise, was the mining of coal. The 1844 map shows an area called Coal Pit along a track a few yards before Hothersall Lane, but on the other side. The track concerned had some almshouses immediately to the right, then about a hundred yards from the road was a trial borehole and some buildings. However, nothing further has been found about the project, but one can imagine how differently the town might have developed with a mining community in the area of the Corporation Arms and Woodville School, now Hillside Autistic Centre.

The building of the two cotton mills was a death blow to the handloom weaving industry situated mainly in King Street and Newtown. However, it would seem the weavers involved were quite happy to move into the mills, providing most of the initial labour. However, in 1862 the Victoria Mill was opened adjacent to the railway line to the quarry, about 200 yards past the goods yard. Then in 1874 Queen's Mill opened, but being situated the far side of Stone Bridge its influence on Berry Lane was marginal. This expansion in the cotton mill trade meant that much of the required labour force had to come from outside Longridge. As people began to be drawn in from outlying areas so a demand for dwelling houses quickly arose. It was in the decade between 1860 and 1870 that various side streets began to appear off Berry Lane and much of the land adjacent to this road itself was built upon. The short streets such as Brewery Street, Chapel Street and Stanley Street were quickly completed, but longer ones including Mersey Street, Humber Street and Severn Street developed much more slowly.

Whilst the properties on the side streets consisted of densely packed terraced houses, there was much more variety on Berry Lane as the years progressed. Quick to anticipate that Berry Lane was in the ascendancy was the Independent Church of Christ. It bought part of the field Little Croft and built an impressive stone church which opened on 21st August 1865. Particularly noticeable are the two pinnacles forming part of the front of the building. A Congregational church, its first minister the Reverend William Booth also had built the residence opposite, "The Manse". Fully aware of the value of educating the young he had added, only a year later, a school room behind the church. Both this and "The Manse" were to his own designs. The school quickly outgrew the room's capacity so that only two years later a much larger building was started. Its success continued and following the 1880 Education Act, making primary education compulsory, it became the alternative for parents who did not want to send their children to either the Anglican or Roman Catholic schools.

Also within the confines of the field 112 (see diagram 2), but not built until 1884, is the Methodist Church which is shown on the 1892 map as a Methodist Chapel (Wesleyan). It cost £1400 and seated 175 and was the third building in the town to house this movement. The previous Methodist building is now a private house, but easily recognisable as a chapel. It was in Calfcote Lane and called itself Mount Zion Wesleyan Chapel.

It would seem sensible to stay with religion and deal with the building of St. Paul's Church. Considering that much of the land on the south side of Berry Lane had been owned by the then Chapel of St. Lawrence, it would seem natural that this church would have taken up some of its own property. However, prolonged disagreement over some twenty years as to whether to build it resulted in most of the land having been sold. Therefore, when it was finally decided in 1886 that a second church was necessary, little of the parish's own land was left. However, the generosity of a Mr Robert Smith, now owner of land including field 107, enabled the church's construction to commence that year with completion in 1890 of a large building seating over 500. Photographs taken before the addition of the tower in 1937 show how much the tower and main entrance enhanced its appearance.

The south side of the lane above the railway line became an area full of public buildings. Below the Congregational Church only the Durham Ox Public House, built about the same time, separated it from the rival Church of England schools. First was a girls school erected in 1865 and extended in 1878. In 1885 Robert Smith, mentioned above, built a boys school to replace one opposite St. Lawrence Church on Lower Lane.
Moving down Berry Lane, still on the same side, is the imposing building built in 1880 to house the Longridge Industrial Co-operative Society's Central Stores and Co-operative Hall. The land had been sold by the parish church for £323-12-8d. From the conveyance we find that

the area of the plot was 2157 square yards, about half an acre. This document indicates that at that time Longridge was in the Diocese of Manchester.

Looking up Berry Lane from near Humber Street
On the left in this approx. 1910 view the first awning is at Longridge Co-operative Society's Tailoring Department. The next one belongs to the Post Office. Two doors further along is a corner shop Bell's Stores, with the hoardings for Turner's Drapery nearby at number.16. Across the top of Berry Lane is part of the original Dog Inn with an adjacent lower building thought to be its brewhouse. on the right-hand side the various prominent buildings still extant today can be identified

The history of the Co-operative Movement in Longridge is the subject of another chapter in this book. But just one bit of information; large as it is the Co-operative Hall would have fitted twice over inside Crampoaks Mill with room to spare.

Before Berry Lane began to be developed the main place where one found retailers was the area at the top of the town, especially King Street and Market Place. There were found the grocers, butchers, drapers etc., along with a weekly market. As properties began to spread along Berry Lane rival shops began to appear. Also some traders decided to transfer their businesses hoping for a more lucrative return. Nonetheless the original centre continued in the ascendancy until the last quarter of the nineteenth century. Even then it continued to be an important shopping centre and offered far more choice to the drinker.

By the time we reach the last decade of the last century Berry Lane has very few gaps in the buildings. The 1892 map shows a couple at the lower end on the north side and the length between the Co-operative Hall and the railway. These gaps were the edges of fields and behind almost all of the buildings on the south side were open fields. The same was true along parts of the opposite side. Luckily today there still is open ground in several places, the field adjacent to St. Paul's church, the recreation ground and Towneley Gardens. But it could have been very different. A hand drawn map has recently come to light which is entitled "Layout of Cricket Field 1880". Overdrawn on this diagram is a road system covering what is now the recreation ground. Barclay Road extends right through to Kestor Lane. Parallel to it and between it and the railway is St. Lawrence Road, also linking Berry Lane and Kestor Lane. Barclay road has several side roads and Clarence Street becomes a through road. Complete details can be seen from the diagram. A slightly later map from around the turn of the century that is the property of St. Paul's church shows Towneley Road as a through road and joining Derby Road where Towneley Road West is today. Warwick Street was to have two short cul-de-sacs on the south side and Derby Road an extra three on the same side as Fleet Street.

Meanwhile on the other side of Berry Lane proposals around 1880 were for three roads parallel to Mersey Street that would link through to Green Lane. However, concern about health and disease in close packed housing meant the plans were dropped. A start had been made on the first street Irwell Street, resulting in a handful of properties at each end numbered 1 and 3 and 111, 113, 115. The other streets were to have been called Ribble Street and Calder Street. The former's proposed location can be recognised where there is a gap in the housing between numbers 14 and 16. Church Street is the site of the latter.

Nowadays Berry Lane is very much the home of vehicular traffic. A century ago the animal reigned supreme. In addition to horses, there were regular movements of cattle and sheep either to the market or the slaughterhouse. The latter was built around this time on a field with the unusual name Botch Collock, along Chapel Street and just past the end of the houses. Animals were tethered in the field now used by the Church Of England Primary School. The business belonged to John Sanderson, one of a line of butchers in the town of that surname. His granddaughter can recall cattle ambling down Chapel Street. The business continued until the 1950s.

It is now time to move into this century and to first look at the brief spell up to the First World War. A Barrett's Trade Directory dated 1901 lists twenty two shops in Berry Lane plus the Co-operative Hall. Only two of the shops were grocers, out of an amazing total of twenty one grocers in the whole town. On the other hand there were six drapers. One James Gray advertised himself as Draper, Tailor and Ironmonger; perhaps he made suits of armour!

Only two properties are still following the same trade almost a century later. Number 71 has continued throughout as a newsagent and stationer. Fifty years ago it was also a Catholic Repository. The other one is the Post Office, built around 1880 and replacing one in King Street. It is now part of a terrace of four, but initially only the centre pair were built. Very early on the Post Office was in the front room of number 26, before moving to number 24 with the postmaster residing in 26. A lady who provided a good deal of useful information about Berry Lane was born there in the early part of this century. It was her grandfather who built the extension that is now an estate agent. Both this building and number 28 have had a varied history, worth looking at in some detail later.

Whilst we would have little difficulty recognising pre-First World War Berry Lane, there were numerous differences from today. It was probably still cobbled and almost all the traffic would have been horsedrawn. In the winter hundreds of house chimneys in the town would have added to the smoke from the four cotton mills and a couple of foundries in Higher Lane (now Inglewhite Road). On a wet and gloomy day things must have appeared pretty dismal. The 1910 Bradshaw timetable shows that the railway line was busy, with nine trains each way on weekdays and a late one Thursdays and Saturdays only. Coincidentally this late train left Preston at 10.50pm the exact time that the last bus does nowadays. On Sundays Longridge only saw three trains, but many other branch lines at the time had no trains on that day. Eleven sidings were in use in the goods yard, one of which served a large goods shed.

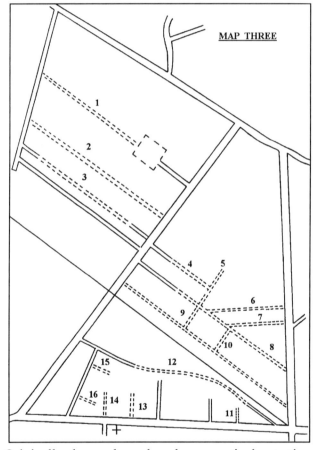

MAP THREE

Roads Proposed but Never Built

1. Calder Street (Church Street part of)
2. Ribble Street
3. Irwell Street (Short stretch built at either end)
4. Clarence Street (Short stretch built)
5. Oxford Street
6. Admarch Street
7. Bache Street
8. Barclay Road(Short stretch built)
9. St. Lawrence Road
10. Buck Street
11. Astley Street
12. Towneley Road (Short stretch at either end, and lower portion now Townley Road West)
13. Clifton Parade
14. Clare Street
15. Cross Street
16. Brown Street

Originally the road numbered consecutively starting at the top on the south side, reaching 37 at the bottom. This continued from the opposite corner and finished up at number 66, now number 2 and part of the Lloyds Trustee Savings Bank. This was altered to the present figures,

12

with a few minor changes later, in the last few years before the Great War. Very probably it was at the same time as the change from Pitt street to Preston Road took place regarding the road at the bottom. The corner property at that end on either side were numbered into Preston Road, only to return in the mid 1950s when that gave way to Inglewhite and Derby Roads.

It was at the turn of the century that a Mr. Joe Fletcher, noted for his unusual building adornments elsewhere in the town, built the properties 84 to 90. At first floor level the windows are arched whilst the stonework is decorated with terracotta tiles, causing a rather foreign looking appearance. The last of the premises was for many years owned by the Mercer family, motor engineers, coach operators and cycle dealers. The first Longridge telephone exchange was in one of the rooms, whilst a friend recalls visiting her dentist in the same building. Much more recently, for a brief spell in the early 1990s, one could visit the "Chatterbox Café" at the back. I am sure we can all suggest some people who ought to have felt very much at home there!

The outbreak of the First World War had the same profound effect on Longridge as any other town or village. In the course of his book Joe Till describes recruiting meetings held on Tootle Heights, accompanied by a photograph taken in 1915. By the end of the war over six hundred Longridge men had served in the armed forces, nearly one hundred of whom died. The exodus can be seen by comparing the shops and businesses operating in 1913 with those in 1917. The Anglican and Roman Catholic churches took little time in deciding how to commemorate those from their congregations who had fallen. By contrast Longridge Urban District Council dithered, dallied and eventually did nothing. Ideas had included mounting a captured German gun on Tootal Heights, the opening of a restaurant at that site, or various ideas of a practical nature. However, it appears feelings in the village were not content with this lack of a memorial, so in 1925 it decided to hold a public meeting. The Chairman at the time, Mr. N. J. Swarbrick, expressed his disappointment at the small attendance, but the meeting went ahead and there was a general consensus of agreement to provide a recreation ground along the lines of the one opened in Chipping to honour that village's dead. Several plots of land were considered, then in the following May the fields that now form the recreation ground were bought from William and Albert Sanderson for £1740, the same family that had built the slaughterhouse. The park was open by the following year and a footpath was included to link Berry Lane and Kestor Lane.

Postcard of Berry Lane taken near Church Street c.1930
The first shop is Jean's, a Ladies Outfitter. Where the fence and wall project outwards is the proposed site for Ribble Street. Below there, Turner's Drapery and on the near corner of Irwell Street, Foley's Grocers. Opposite it is the premises of W. Prestwick and Sons, Ironmongers and Furnisher. Then comes the Post Office and much further down Crampoaks Mill and chimney. One wonders why the mill was built at an angle to the road.

An enclosed area for children complete with a mainly wooden shelter was added later. The shelter was to suffer at the hands of vandals, the plaque attached was lost or stolen, it soon fell into disuse and has been demolished for many years. However, the fine wrought iron gates at either end of the park, albeit in need of some paint, remain as a suitable memorial. Although properly called Kestor Lane Recreation Ground many refer to it as the "Berry Lane Rec." due to its proximity to the main street.

Before the war motor vehicles had made some inroads into the complete reliance on horses. This take-over proceeded apace in the nineteen-twenties, so that photographs of Berry Lane taken at that time often contain interesting early vehicles. It must have been about then that the cobbles disappeared under tarmacadam. By 1930 the bus service to Preston had so reduced the number of people travelling by train that the passenger service was withdrawn in the middle of that year. But if a proposal discussed by L.U.D.C in 1919 had been carried out one could have travelled on rails from the centre of Preston to the centre of Blackburn. The idea was to join the outer limit of each town's tramway by a route running via Longridge and Ribchester. It came to nothing, but the thought of seeing trams clanking up the steep part of Berry Lane has some appeal.

Nowadays when we say such and such a road is a busy one we usually mean with vehicles. But in this between-the-wars period, it was the large numbers of pedestrians. Busy times included the surge towards Cramp Oaks or Victoria Mills in time for the 7am start. Not only the chatter, but the sound of scores of pairs of clogs as the weavers hurried to beat the hooter. A couple of hours later large numbers of smaller clogs rang out on the pavement as hundreds of children converged on the three schools. Some of these workers and children would have walked considerable distances from outlying areas.

The appearance of Berry Lane changed here and there during this between-the- wars era. In the early stages there was a photographer's wooden cabin on the raised land adjacent to Humber Street. Across the road another cabin offered fish and chips. The latter was swept away when the Co-operative Society used the site to build its new grocery store, opened in 1933. Four years later the tower addition to St. Paul's church was finished. Although it was, of course, some distance form Berry Lane, the closure of the Victoria Mill in 1936 would have had some effect on it. Obviously there was not only a drop in the numbers of people on the move twice a day, but also loss of trade for the shopkeepers. The effect of the severe recession of the early 1930's on Longridge is a subject yet to be tackled.

The subject of Longridge during World War Two is dealt with in another chapter of this book. Suffice to say here that none of the buildings were damaged or destroyed by enemy bombs. Moving on to post war times, I have divided this period into two spells of around twenty five years. By the early 1970s some fundamental changes had occurred. The most significant was the mill's closure in 1959. The loss of a way of life for many, it was a major change in the activity in Berry Lane. The mill site was bought by the Warwick Street firm Willacy and Baker. Any plans to utilise the main building were discarded when it was found the building was dangerous. The biggest task was the demolition of the massive concrete platform that had supported the mill's steam engine. Weaving sheds at the rear of the site escaped demolition, being fairly late additions to the works. Another casualty was the lodge with its dark, steaming water. No doubt the goldfish it contained were found homes elsewhere. This spot was an ideal place for the substitution of petrol and diesel tanks for a filling station. A garage was opened near the pumps, in front of the ex-weaving sheds. Briefly the sheds became a hatchery for chicks before changing to their present use as a vehicle repair shop.

Part of the mill site became the first cut-price grocery store in the town. Many residents no doubt remember "Whittakers" who moved to this purpose-built premises from number 82 a little further down. The premises changed hands in due course with extensions following and the acquisition of the lower end of the goods yard for a car park. The railway yard had ceased operation in late 1967 and the tracks were lifted the next year. To accommodate the new road to link new housing estates planned to the north of the lane the road level at the site of the level crossing was raised around three feet lessening the slope down. If the Ordnance Survey map of 1975 is correct Willows Park Lane began at Berry Lane in the first instance, but was altered obviously at a later date. By this time the Civic Hall and both Park and Towneley Houses were in use. The railway station buildings were retained as offices, so one walks along part of the old platform if you want to visit "The Longridge Homing Society", "St. John's Ambulance Brigade", "Ribble Valley Borough Council Office", or "Longridge Town Council Office". For many years the Homing Society's pigeons were taken by train to the point of release.

The upper half of Berry Lane also saw several major alterations and changes in this period. The Church of England Schools lost their senior pupils to Longridge High School in 1959 and the whole complex became a primary school. The school to the rear of the Congregational Church continued as a primary school only, until the County Primary School was built in 1969. The rearmost part of the old school premises have since been demolished, to be replaced by houses in traditional stone.

The largest private house in the lane was at the very top north end, the mansion called "The Limes". Before dealing with post-war alterations a brief look at the premises' history is well worth while. Its date of construction is uncertain, but very probably was in the 1880s. Suggestions that 1871 and 1881 census entries of a house called "The Oaks" is this property under an earlier name, may be red herrings. It could possibly have been number 6 which later became "Bank House" when owned by the District Bank. The first definite reference to "The Limes" is in an 1889 directory. A James Kay junior was in residence and this family of cotton traders resided here until the end of The First World War. They were followed by John or Jack Smith who was in the same field of business, making frequent journeys to the Cotton Exchange in Manchester. Two sons called Wilfrid and Dennis were born during his stay at "The Limes". Some older residents in Longridge may well recall being invited to play with these lads in the extensive gardens. Such halcyon days are long since gone, after being empty for some while the main part of the site was bought in 1947 by L.U.D.C. for its office premises. In due course the rose garden became the premises of the Surveyor's Department of L.C.C. which remain today. Then in 1964 a new local library was built in the old grounds, to replace the building on the corner of Market Street. Stocking eight thousand books and including a reference section, it was a big improvement on its predecessor. In recent years there have been regular art displays in the library which is also used on occasions for lectures. The original "Limes" building continued as local government offices until the 1974 reorganisation. Some years use as offices for solicitors, accountants and the like was followed by the change to its current use as a pre-school nursery and providing after school care for five to eleven year olds. Thus for only just over half its life has it been a private house.

Having strayed well beyond the 1970s toward the end of the last paragraph it is time to bring the survey into the last quarter of the century. As we leave the post war period it should be remembered there were far fewer shops then. For example a 1970 photograph shows all the premises between forty-eight and sixty-two as still just houses, highlighting their fine doorways. But nowadays the number of houses along the whole street is a small minority. However, many of the shops and businesses have residences above them. A 1980 survey of Berry Lane properties is revealing when one discovers that relatively few of the shops and businesses operating then still exist today.

Probably the biggest change in this period has been the closure of the Co-operative Hall in 1985. Increased competition locally and the fact that far more people were able to drive into Preston to shop were the main causes. The idea of holding a dividend rather went out of fashion in the 1960s and 1970s, a form of saving particularly associated with the Co-operative Movement. Ironically it is back with a vengeance when we remember how many firms have now introduced points cards. The Co-operative grocery section was retained having by then developed into a supermarket to rival the one operated by Spar. In the early 1980s Arnold Swift and Sons Ltd opened a large bathrooms and kitchens business at the lower end of the road at numbers 73 and 75. The former had once been Pearsons Corn Mill, a big premises extending through to Warwick Street. A fire at this mill was made more vivid to observers by the large number of rats fleeing to escape the flames.

The effects of the free church reorganisation came to Longridge when the Methodist and Congregational Churches combined to become Longridge United Reformed Church in the early 1990s. Both buildings continued in use initially, but after considerable modernisation, including the front entrance on Berry Lane, the latter building was retained. The Methodist building was sold and after a spell as a children's clothes shop became Longridge Teaching Centre, offering various further education courses. Within the last five years a Medical Centre has been opened on land behind the present Co-operative. This centre contains several of the facilities, particularly General Practice, previously found at the town's other Medical Centre in King Street.

The chemist's shop closed down soon after the changes took place. The business was transferred to number 40 Berry Lane close to the new centre.

With so much emphasis in towns and villages up and down the country on retaining features from the past, it was thus a disappointment to many when Church Street's setts were replaced by tarmacadam in 1999.

I have endeavoured so far to show how Berry Lane has altered across the years, the growth of housing, the introduction of businesses and its importance in the town. To conclude I want to have a brief look at some of the properties and their past, hopefully reminding long term Longridgians of shops they once used for a different purpose than they would nowadays.

One premises that has had quite a varied history is number 43, presently the Youth Club. This frontage is the outcome of it starting its life as a mineral water company called Ellis Wilkinson. Erected in the late nineteenth century it had a wide archway to enable horse drawn carts to be loaded inside. About seventy years ago it had become a small market for greengrocery and fish with a laundry at the rear. The latter is better known for having housed Mr. Lawrence Bond's workshop during the early stages of his Bond Minicar development. In 1939 the outbreak of the war resulted in the complex becoming the Auxiliary Fire Service Station and the local telephone switchboard. The fire engine remained here until the purpose built station was opened in Whittingham Road in 1967.

The Towneley Arms owned the park land next to the Youth Club for many years. The hotel's first owner had bought Great Meadow, (the Great Meadow 117 on Map 3) below the railway line. The large hotel was erected some time in the 1840s and in their first flush of enthusiasm the Fleetwood Preston and West Riding Junction Railway not only took over the Preston and Longridge Railway but bought the hotel and renamed it The Longridge Railway Tavern. Within five years the property had to be resold, in due course becoming the Towneley Arms. It is known that the hotel was a useful asset for visitors to the town, being so centrally situated. The land not used for the hotel building, stables and outhouses became a large garden full of trees and shrubs. A bowling green had been laid by the time the 1892 Ordnance Survey map appeared, its outline clearly apparent.

1970 photograph of the District Bank, nearer property once called Rose Cottage, amongst its residents was Hedley Booth.

This 1970 photograph of numbers 6 and 8 Berry Lane was taken by society member Mr. Brian Bamber. The County Bank bought the former some time after the First World War. Prior to that it had been resided in by a Mr. Southworth and at another stage was home to a Miss Alston, headmistress of the Infant School. By 1932 the District Bank had taken over and the premises was known as Bank House. For many years the local manager lived above the premises. After the Bank vacated number 6 it became the premises of J. D. Cliff, Insurance Brokers. It has been empty for the last 4 years. Number 8 was Rose Cottage for many years and was built in the last quarter of the nineteenth century. A hundred years ago Robert Smith owner of the Victoria Mill occupied the property. Following him the family of Hedley Booth of ironmonger fame lived here for over forty years. After other private occupants it was bought by the District Bank to replace its neighbouring premises. The area between the pavement and the properties had once been small front gardens. Number 8 was demolished a few months after this photograph was taken and replaced by the present bank building.

Moving into this century a photo from the Edwardian era reveals that the Longridge Cycling Club had one of the rooms as its headquarters. One of the best known of its victuallers was a Mr. Henry Handley. He advertised in the 1917 Barrett directory "The Towneley Arms, posting house, good stabling, bowling green. Telephone number 16". A lifelong Longridge resident can recall the period when Mr. Handley raised horses for pulling funeral hearses. The Towneley Arms continues to operate as a public house, but the bowling green initially passed to the L.U.D.C., who then requested the Royal British Legion to operate it. The garden area continues to flourish as Towneley Gardens, public conveniences being added. A triangle of land furthest from the road was taken up by a wing of Towneley House.

One realises how reliant householders were on coal when the 1917 trade directory lists five coal merchants in Longridge. The companies' offices were at the end of the railway goods yard land now occupied by Towneley Parade. The only exception was Thomas Banks Co. who had premises on the opposite side of the road adjacent to the station. This yard was served by a siding just above and outside the confines of the level crossing. The offices were in small two storey building next to the railway's signal box.

Whereas many of Berry Lane's houses became shops, just a few premises have gone the other way. One such is number 5 which in its very early days, i.e. the 1870s and 1880s, was the premises of one J. Crossley Boot and Shoe Maker. (How many of us can remember having had shoes actually made for us in these days of mass production?). By 1917 it was run by Thomas Willacy a confectioner and it was to remain in this trade until it ceased to be a shop in 1980. It continued to be run by members of this family and later became known as Willacy's Toffee Shop. The 1948 Barrett's Trade Directory also includes Willacy and Baker, Motor Engineers and James Willacy, Blacksmith. Horses are supposed to be sweet toothed, so one would expect they preferred to be shod at this smithy.

Number 7, next door, has had a varied career. The earliest record found is for 1889 when it was a fish shop, by the turn of the century it was Turner a Draper in residence who in 1905 moved into number sixteen where he and his family continued in drapery for over sixty years. Meanwhile number 7 may have reverted to a house as it is not listed in the 1913 and 1917 directories.

1970 photograph of numbers 1, 3 and 5 note Willacy's famous toffee shop (number five)

A 1970 photograph of numbers 1, 3 and 5 in shadow. The first, currently up for sale, has had spells as a house and others as a shop. For many years it was called Empire House as a close look at the photograph reveals. Number 3's small size is due to it having once been an archway to give access to buildings on Market Place. It appears to have been a private house throughout. Whilst number 5 is now also a house, it was a shop for many years, notably Willacy's Toffee Shop as in the photograph. (Further details are outlined in the text about number 5)

For much of the period between the wars it was where William Higginson made clogs, boots and shoes. He was followed by Hubert Crook who had his chemist business here until 1943. We catch up with him again at number 99. It seems to have reverted to a house again but by 1968 was a showrooms for C. A. Burton Electrical Engineers. Much more recently it was a health shop, now only open part time as an Allergy Clinic.

We might as well remain on this side of the road and call in at number 23. If we had done so in 1871 it would have been to meet Mr. Woolley and his wife who were master and mistress at the Congregational School. This property was called Regent House until about 1975, presumably so christened by a Prince Albert devotee. But back to its uses, in the 1880s, it was a Milliner and Dressmaker; after which firstly Walton, then Richmond both of whom were tailors. In a 1932 directory it is listed as the Manchester and City Bank, open Mondays, Thursdays and Saturdays. Quite a few older Longridge residents remember it best as the showrooms for the Longridge Gas Company and its nationalised successor. In the late 1960s, it became a ladies hairdresser and then more recently a take-away premises.

One of the bigger companies now operating in Berry Lane is that of Arnold Swift and Son Ltd whose ironmongery, hardware and garden business occupies what were numbers 53 to 57. The first purchase was number 55 which had been an ironmongery for over fifty years. For much of that time it was run by the Prestwich family, although many recall it as "Gertie's" when a Mrs. Hewitt and her daughter of that name were the proprietors, until Swifts began in 1968. Number 53 followed later having been in its time a newsagent and stationer under Crook's, then H. & M. Corbridge who also ran a lending library and finally Duerden's. Number 57 continued separately for quite somewhile. In 1981 it was an optician who had succeeded a hairdresser. Then in 1982 it became a confectioners.

The final property on the odd side is number 99, shut since January 1995 and scheduled along with 97 to be demolished to improve traffic movement at the junction with Inglewhite and Derby Roads. This pair of properties stand out, partly because of the black and white paint over the stonework, but by being two or three feet higher at the eaves than the stretches of terracing that adjoin them. To many lifelong dwellers in Longridge it is still called Dagger's corner. This is due to the first owner being James Dagger of Goosnargh a Corn and Provision Merchant, as well as a schoolmaster. The Anglican church had sold the land to a Thomas Pearce in December 1863 which Dagger then bought on which to build a Provender business. His wife had a grocery business in the shop part of 99 (originally number 37), the bone crushing, corn and provision business being in the rear and taking up the first part of Derby Road. The big double doors led through into a small courtyard with a stable. Much of the material was stored at first floor level, for which an entry door accommodating a crane with a wooden jib lifted items from the road below. By 1924 this site had become the grocery and general store of a George Marsh, then in 1943 Hubert Crook moved his chemists from number 7. More recently it was also a chemist under S. & C. Brierley; then briefly United Chemists (Co-op) who transferred to their present location near Stone Bridge.

Number 82 has been one of the more varied evens. There is a record of it being Critchley Druggists (not a pharmacy) in the 1920s, by 1932 Harry Edmundson a Tailor and Draper owned it, followed by Harry Mercer in the same lines recorded as being there in 1948. Twenty years afterwards it was both a Washeteria and the Bare Dry Cleaners, following a fairly short period as Whittaker's cut-price store mentioned earlier. In 1981 it was still a Laundrette but also accommodated Visions Boutique. Nowadays a haberdasher who in recent years were first above the off-licence at number 20, then opposite there in the upper end shop in the old Co-op building. Since moving to 82 the owners have introduced a second-hand business on the first floor.

A few doors away at number 64 the first record is for 1913 when it was Holden's both a boot and shoe maker and draper. One source suggests this was the Henry Holden founder of the Auctioneers in Warwick Street. However, the 1948 Barrett's Trade Directory has Henry Holden and Sons (Established 1890) Auctioneers, Valuers, and Hotel Valuers, Poultry Sale every Monday, with offices at number 80. At number 64 in 1948 was housed the Ministry of Labour Office managed by a Mr. C. Bilsborough. Another type of labour was then appropriate as it became "Babyland". Conroy and Jones had a longish spell next with their rather unusual mix of office stationery and toys. In recent years it was briefly a shop for material and it is now a flower shop.

Some residents recall going to the private school established in 1924 on the upper floor of number 56, which was run by the sisters Misses Josephine and Winifred Smith. Unlike many such schools it did not fold, but transferred to College Villas and we now pass it every time we go into Preston as it formed the basis of the "Woodlands School" opposite the end of Cromwell Road.

1970 photograph of numbers 56 to 62, now all shops
Numbers 56 to 62 in 1970, when this block and that to its right, numbers 48 to 54, were all private houses. Before and for part of the second world war numbers 56 and 58 were the grocers run by Annie Pomfret. Number 60 was Bell's Stores in the 1917 Barrett Trade Directory. Nowadays all four properties are businesses, mainly fashion shops or hairdressers.

Number 28, mentioned briefly before, was a fish and chip shop from before World War One with firstly Jas Eccles, then John Riding. In 1932 it was still a John Riding but now a sweet shop. Fish were back in the next decade when T. Singleton and his wife had a fishmongery, fruiterers, sold flowers and would make up wreaths on request. By 1968 it had become D. Forrest, a ladies hairdresser, only for the men to get the upper hand, as it has been a barber's shop for the last two decades. The first floor rooms are an accountant's office.

At the other end of the block there is now a Building Society coupled with an Estate Agent. Until around 1975 it had been the Co-operative

Society Greengrocery, with a warehouse for mobile shops at the rear. For much of the first half of this century it had been Prestwick and Sons (not to be confused with Prestwich at number 55) which in 1917 was a furniture dealer, ironmonger and leather goods business. Still trading in 1948 the firm also described itself as an Agricultural Engineer.

Many more premises have had similar histories of several owners and various trades, but those detailed above enable us to see something of the changes Longridge has seen in this road alone. Several real characters of earlier decades have been mentioned and one could add Hedley Booth proprietor in the 1920s at Prestwick and Sons, Mrs Foley who is recalled as a rather strict manageress of Foley's Grocers (at numbers 18 and 20) yet was very happy to deal with the collection money from the Penny a Week Red Cross collecting in the last war. How many now recall Jimmy Sharples the Bellman who, in the days before radio, went along the street in a two wheeled donkey cart, stopping every seventy yards or so to pass on local news? The Bellman was a long established post and is mentioned in several local newspaper reports from the nineteenth century. In 1901 he is listed as David Prestwich Billposter and Bellman. As far as one knows there were never any of the large type of advertising hoardings in Berry Lane or any on the ends of houses.

The continued rise in the number of retail premises in Berry Lane has taken its toll on the shops in other streets, although people choosing to shop in Preston will also have had a bearing. The decline in roads such as King Street, Market Place, Inglewhite and Derby roads is most noticeable in the food sector. Until around forty years ago grocers, confectioners, butchers and bakers could be found in some quantity elsewhere than on Berry Lane. Nowadays many of these are either houses or in such outlets as hairdressing. Stone Bridge has managed to continue as a small shopping area, assisted by the amount of industry in that locality. But although Berry Lane has fared a good deal better, apart from the two supermarkets few of its shops are food retailers either. However, there have appeared quite a few take-aways in the last decade or so. The variety of shops is encouraging so that most needs can be met. However, one has to add that at the time of writing, May 1999, seven shops and a commercial property were empty, several having been for sale for well over a year. It is too soon to discover whether a new supermarket opened in Inglewhite Road three months ago will have an adverse effect. But if the numbers milling around Berry Lane on the Extravaganza nights is anything to go by there is not too much to worry about.

In a few months time we will reach the beginning of the new millennium. Berry Lane will see at least one change at the time with the installation of the Millennium Cross on the raised strip of ground opposite the Towneley Arms. We have been looking at our subject over a period of around one hundred and fifty years. The survey has not been done as just a detailed survey of the road and its buildings. Rather to examine its importance as Longridge has grown and developed during this time. It is intriguing to wonder what Berry Lane will be like in 2150 after a further such period of time.

BIBLIOGRAPHY

A History Of Longridge and Its People. J.M.Till. Carnegie Publishing 1993.

The Preston and Longridge Railway. N.Parker. Oakwood Press, 1972

Berry Lane. Longridge and District Local History Society. 1983.

I made extensive use of maps covering the last one hundred and sixty years:-

The Tithe Map of Alston dated 1837.
The Tithe Map of Dilworth dated 1838.
Ordnance Survey six inch to a mile and 1/2500 scale maps that appeared at various dates from 1844 until 1991.

I received much useful information from many local residents to whom I am very grateful, particularly:-
Mrs. Nora Pinder, Mrs. Margaret Swarbrick, Mr. Glyn Baker and Mr. Edgar Willacy.

Finally my grateful thanks to Mr. Daniel Lamont for checking the text for grammatical error and my daughter Frances Keeney for the typing of the text.

LONGRIDGE INDUSTRIAL CO-OPERATIVE SOCIETY

Ronald Seed

The Co-operative Movement began in 1844 in premises in Toad Lane, Rochdale, with the foundation of the Rochdale Equitable Pioneers' Society, and the movement spread rapidly in Lancashire and Yorkshire.

In Longridge, one of the reasons behind the formation of a local Society was because of the complaints about the high prices being charged in the "Tommy shops", run by the owners of the cotton mills, which mill employees were pressurised to support. Tom Smith says that the Society originated in the quarry of Messrs. Waring Bros. when five men - Thomas Coupe, James Pye, Henry Slinger, William Waring and Isaac Wilkinson - called a meeting, attended by 30 people, at which a Committee of Management was appointed and the Longridge Industrial Co-operative Society was formed, 20 persons joining as members.[1] It was formally established on 24 March 1874 and registered under the Industrial and Provident Societies Act of 1862, which permitted societies to operate their business and trade, but also allowed other pursuits, such as educational activities.

Two cottages in Fell Brow were converted into a shop which was open in the evenings and staffed by the Committee. The amount of trade done for the first year was £1,800 during which time the membership had increased to 146, with share capital to the amount of £601 5s. 11d.[2] A second shop was opened in Pitt Street (Preston Road) in 1876, and a further branch in Lee Street in 1886.

On 16 September 1875, the Committee resolved to open the stores at 8.a.m. instead of 7.30 a.m. and to close at 1 p.m. on Tuesdays. The dividend was to be 1s.9d. in the £ for members and 10d. for non-members. Mr. Joseph Riding was appointed "Shopman" of the Pitt Street Stores at 23s. per week, and Mr. Bamber was commissioned to paint its sign board for 20s. and to fix gas fittings in the store for 23s.6d.

The Committee, whose members included Messrs. Fowler, Harrison, Procter, Pye, Riding and Wilkinson, resolved on 5 October 1875 to meet twice every week, their remuneration to be 6d. per night. At their next meeting, on 11 October, they requested Messrs. Brown and Whiteside to tender for shelving at the Fell Brow and Pitt Street Stores.

Plans were put in hand for a Teaparty to be held early in 1876, and Mr. Robert Allen of Oldham was to be invited to Preside and give an address. The meeting of 29 November passed a lengthy resolution including: That it be held on the last Saturday in January; - That the Choir of Berry Lane Chapel be asked to render their services; - That James Gardner and D. Postlethwaite be asked to sing a few Comic Songs.

On 23 December 1875, the dividend was raised to 1s.10d. in the £ for members and 11d. for non-members.

On 3 February 1876, it was resolved, "That the premises and Shop situate in Pitt Street belonging to Charles Fletcher be taken at a rent of 4s.10d. per week". It was also agreed to "commence the manufacturing of Clogs".

Evidence of increasing trade shows in discussions on insuring the contents of the stores, buying a fire-proof safe and making investments, including 25 shares in the Longridge Co-operative Cotton Manufacturing Company. Concerns with provisions led to a letter being sent to the Co-operative Wholesale Society regarding the bad conditions of apples, and the decision on 3 July 1876, "That the Sale of Butchers meat at the Stores be Discontinued for the present".

It was also agreed, "That we make use of the house now occupied by Mr. Waring, Shopman, as a Coffee and Additional Store Rooms, and the Chairman to inform Mr. Waring of the same and request him to look after another house as soon as convenient".[3]

In 1877, it was decided to merge the Clog and Shoe Departments. W. Clarkson was engaged as foreman Shoemaker at 26s. per week, with Thomas Walmsley at 6s. per week and Thomas Wallbank at 4s.

Plans for a Field Day were put in hand. It was resolved:-

That there be a Field Day for the members of Small Savings Bank, on or about July 14th.

> That Buns and Coffee be provided free to each member;
> That Longridge Brass Band be engaged for the occasion;
> That all Non-members be charged 3d. each admittance to the field;
> That Alston Brass Band be engaged also;
> That 800 Currant Buns be ordered.

When the Committee met on 1 April 1878, a resolution was passed, "That the meeting become 'Special' to consider the advisability of having a Central Stores and Co-operative Hall". Later, a Special Building Committee was elected, consisting of James Hull, Richard Kay, William Coupe, James Whiteside, Thomas Scott and Joseph Bolton.[4]

On 7 October 1878, it was decided to purchase Queen Anne's Bounty Land in Berry Lane from the Church at a cost of £323 12s.8d. Messrs. Longworth and Gardner were appointed architects. On 10 February 1879, a plan was decided upon, with the proviso that the cost of the land, building and fittings should not exceed £2,500. By 26 March, tenders had been received and allocated.

On Saturday 24 May, the ceremonial procession set off from the Fell Brow stores, and the corner-stone was laid at the right-hand front corner of the new building by Mr. Robert Smith of Dilworth House on Dilworth Lane, the builder and owner of Victoria Mill at the top of Mersey Street. A bottle was placed under the stone, containing three local newspapers, a copy of the Society's rules, its latest Quarterly Report and Balance Sheet and the current Co-operative Newspaper.

On 3 December 1879, it was decided to fix an 8-day clock to the front of the building at a cost of £45. In the following February, three members were elected "to wait upon the gentry of the district to solicit subscriptions for the clock fund".

The official opening took place on Saturday, 17 July 1880.

Later, the Central Stores were enlarged to form a building 100ft. in frontage, 80ft. wide and 60ft. high, including a large public room on the top floor able to hold up to 800 people. The extension was opened in October 1888 with a tea party, concert and Ball. They also founded a Savings Bank.

In addition to the General Committee, responsible for the policy, management and trading of the Society and its shops, an Educational Committee was formed, which had oversight of the Library and Reading Room; promoted lectures and classes; started a Debating Society; and organised various welfare and recreational activities in Longridge and the surrounding villages, including the popular Annual Field Day.

Grocery shop, central stores c.1900 (names unknown)

Little is known of the early progress of the Society: a former President borrowed the first Minute Book which would have given much valuable information and its present whereabouts is unknown.

Nevertheless, the venture was clearly successful, as the following figures show:

	Members	Sales	Capital	Dividend
1887	722	£17,000	£7,338	2s.2d. in £
1906	1,133	£34,363	£20,233	2s.6d. in £

Boot and Shoe shop, Central Stores

Left to right J. Rogerson(?), J Hodson, W. Kenworthy (Manager)

By 1911, the departments at the Central Stores were: Grocery and Provisions; Drapery; Tailoring; Furnishing; Clog; Boot and Shoe; Butchering; Baking; and Provender. Branch Stores were described as Preston Road, Stone Bridge (Grocery) and Stone Bridge (Butchery). In that year, Danish Butter cost 1s.6d. per lb. and Sugar 3d. per lb.

Just before the outbreak of the Great War in 1914, the Society was advertising "Choice assorted Chocolates for Christmas from the Co-operative factory at Luton. One pound box at 1s.2d., or purchase special tickets at Grocery Shops at 1d. each and exchange them when you have 14".

That winter, lectures and concerts were curtailed, "owing to the unsettled state of the country", and though the Annual Field Day went ahead in July 1915, it was abandoned for the rest of the War.

By early 1916 there were shortages of some provisions, (Butter is dear, Margarine 1s. per lb.), and the Stone Bridge Butchery shop closed. The Society announced, "We respectfully desire to draw the attention of our Members to the restrictions placed by the Government on the supply of Paper Bags. By returning all Paper Bags suitable for re-use, or by bringing your own Carpet Bags for your commodities, you will not only be helping your Country, but also assisting to curtail the enormous expense created on your own business". Reference was also made to the "depletion of Society staffs for military purposes", though no record has been found of the names of employees who left to serve their country.

Pitt Street Shop

(left to right - R.Rowcroft, J. Clegg (manager)

After the War, the Longridge Urban District Council considered for several years what form a War Memorial for the village should take. It was eventually decided to purchase a field off Kestor Lane for a Recreation Ground. To provide access from Berry Lane, the Society allowed a footpath to be created through its land, which became known as Barclay Road. Opening hours in the early 1920s at the Central Stores were 8.30 a.m. to 7.00 p.m. on Monday and Tuesday, 8.30 a.m. to 12.30 p.m. on Wednesday, 8.30 a.m. to 8.00 p.m. on Thursday and Friday, and 8.00 a.m. to 5.00 p.m. on Saturday.

In 1924, the Society celebrated its Golden Jubilee with the traditional Field Day and Sports on Saturday 12 July, favoured with fine weather. There was also a series of free Tea Parties and Concerts for members in Longridge, Chipping, Knowle Green, Hurst Green, Whitechapel and Goosnargh (where a new Grocery store was opened). Part of the teas consisted of cream puffs and chocolate eclairs, with whipped cream, and members were reminded that these could be bought from the stores for 2d.

A new development, also in Jubilee year, was the purchase of a "Motor Lurry" for £565 10s., though horses continued to be used, and sales of manure raised income until 1951. Still in 1924, Best House Coal was 2s.5d. per cwt., Seconds and Kitchen Nuts were 2s.1d., both ready bagged. Loose loads were 1d. per cwt. less, and collection in your own cart saved 2d. per cwt.

1910. Prize - winning cattle at the Society's Slaughterhouse.
(left to right, T. Watson, F. McCoskery (manager), R. Skelton)

In 1930 the General Committee noted with regret the depression of work in the cotton industry in Longridge, which was affecting sales. However, they invested for the future in a "Butchery Hawking Van - as regards hygienic, commodious, equipment and being serviceable, we believe that none others are at present in any way comparable".

In the Grocery, Danish Butter was 1s.7d. per lb., (virtually the same as in 1911), Lancashire Lard was 8½ per lb. and Flour 1s.7d. for 14lbs.
In 1932 in Furnishing, Deck Chairs were 3s.9d., Vacuum Flasks 1s.3d. Garden Hose 3d. per foot and a 10 inch Lawn Mower with a Grass Box 30s. Electric Irons and Electric Fires were both 9s. and Vacuum Cleaners 5 guineas. A new line was Wireless Sets, with Ecko, Pye, Atlas, Ultra and Ferranti as makes to choose from.

The grocery trade in the 1930s was very different from the experience of today's supermarkets. Almost all provisions were bought by the Co-op. in bulk. King Edward potatoes came in railway wagons from Lincolnshire; flour, sugar and pulses by the sack; butter in one cwt. barrels. Bulky items were first hoisted upstairs and then fed down chutes to where they were weighed up into packages at the counters.

Through the 1930s, much reorganisation took place. In 1933 a new Grocery and Butchery shop was built in Berry Lane and the Central Stores were refurbished.

The Tailoring Dept. transferred to the Drapery Dept. and the Clog Dept. moved to the former Butchery Dept. In 1935, though the closure of Victoria Mill affected the Society's trade, a new Butchery Branch was opened at 9 Whittingham Road. In 1938, a new Confectionery Dept. included a cafe for light refreshments, with Hot Meat and Potato Pies and Fruit Tarts featured in the announcement of the opening.

1910. Stone Bridge Butchery Branch.
(left to right, T. Watson, R. Skelton, J. Gardner, (Father Christmas), F. McCoskery.

Inflation was not a major factor, as the Society's advertisements reveal: 1917 Loaves 6d. and 11½. 1928 2lb. loaf 4d. 1936 New Brown Bread 3d. for 1lb. loaf, White Bread 2lb. loaf 3½., 4lb. loaf 7d.

In the late 1930s, the Society bought the Wigan Coal and Cannel business in Longridge and then had its own waggons to bring coal direct from the collieries to the Longridge sidings. The waggons were requisitioned by the Government in 1940 and were never returned after the War, though compensation was paid. Coal was delivered to members for the duration by horse-drawn carts.

During the War, 18 employees left the Society to serve in the Armed Forces or to become Bevin Boys. All returned safely after hostilities ceased. There was some opposition from members when Ivy Leeming, the first female assistant to work in the Grocery Dept. was appointed, the objection being to "taking men's jobs". All the staff who remained carried out firewatching duties on a rota basis every night and some joined the Home Guard or the Fire Service. In 1942, members were invited to register for rations.

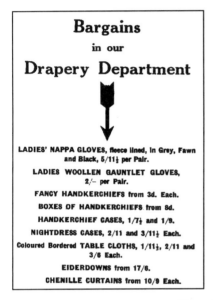

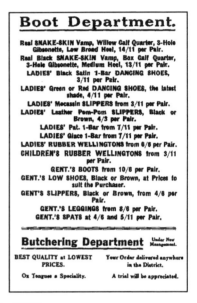

Bargains in 1935

Both buying and selling were restricted by war-time legislation and rationing, and there were transport difficulties.

Educational activities were hampered by travel and black-out restrictions. Owing to National Emergency regulations, Field Days could not be held, but the Annual Children's Ball continued, and in 1942 almost 500 young people attended the Holiday Week Juvenile Ball and took part in the Longridge Holidays-at-Home programme.

In the same year, the Bakery was extended, and the night and day shifts were able to produce welcome supplies of bread as other food shortages appeared through attacks on convoys during the Battle of the Atlantic. The quantities of raw materials allocated were based on pre-war usage.

Grocery Department.

Butter
DANISH   .........................*O.P. per lb.
EMPIRE   .........................*O.P. ,, ,,

Lard
ENGLISH REFINED ....10d. per lb.
HOME RENDERED ....11d. ,, ,,

Bacon a Speciality
HOME-CURED   ....1/- per lb.

Hams
HOME-CURED   ....1/6 ,, ,,
DANISH.
BACON   .........................*O.P. ,, ,,
GAMMON   .........................*O.P. ,, ,,

Sugar
.............................From 2¾d. per lb.

Canned Meats
OX AND LUNCH TONGUES.
AND OTHER COMMODITIES FOR THE
HOUSEHOLD,
CAN BE HAD AT ALL OUR GROCERY
DEPARTMENTS,
AT REASONABLE MARKET PRICES.

Tinned Fruits
(ALL SIZES).
APRICOTS,
    Sliced or Whole ...from 4½d. to 1/2 per tin
FRUIT SALAD .... ,, 6d. ,, 1/4 ,,
PINEAPPLES,
    Cubes or Sliced .... ,, 4d. ,, 8½d. ,,
GRAPEFRUIT ..... ,, 4½d. ,, 8d. ,,
PEACHES .... ,, 5d. ,,11d. ,,
PEARS .... ,, 5d. ,, 1/- ,,

* O.P. denotes Open Price.

Jams and Marmalade

	1s.	2s.	3s
APRICOT ....7d.	1/1		
APRICOT & APPLE ....6d.	10½d.		
BLACK CURRANT ....8d.	1/2		
BLACK CURRANT AND			
APPLE ....6½d.	1/-		
BLACKBERRY ....6½d.	1/-		
BLACKBERRY & APPLE ...6d.	10½d.		
DAMSON ....6½d.	1/-		
DAMSON (Stoneless) ....6½d.	1/-		
DAMSON & APPLE ....6d.	10½d.		
GOOSEBERRY ....6d.	10½d.		
GOOSEBERRY & PLUM .....6d.	10½d.		
GRAPEFRUIT ....6d.	11d.		
GREENGAGE ....6½d.	1/-		
MARMALADE ....6d.	11d.	1/3
,, (Lemon) ......7d.	1/-		
,, (Lemon Jelly) 7½d.	1/1½		
,, (Orange Jelly) 7d.	1/-		
,, (Ginger) ......7d.	1/-		
,, (Grape Fruit			
Jelly) ....8d.	1/3		
PLUM & APPLE ....6d.	10d.		
PLUM (VICTORIA) ....6½d.	1/-		
RED PLUM ....6d.	10½d.		
RASPBERRY ....8d.	1/2		
RASPBERRY & APPLE ......6½d.	1/-	1/3
RASPBERRY & GOOSE-			
BERRY ....7d.	1/-		
RASPBERRY & RED			
CURRANT ....7d.	1/-		
RED CURRANT ....7d.	1/-		
STRAWBERRY (all Brands) 8d.	1/2		
STRAWBERRY & APPLE ...6½d.	1/-	1/5
STRAWBERRY & GOOSE-			
BERRY ....7d.	1/-	1/6
STRAWBERRY & PLUM ....7d.	1/-		

Price list, Christmas and New Year, 1936-37

Meanwhile, 3-piece suites in Moquette, Rexine or Connolly's Hide were available without coupons, from 30 guineas to 55 guineas, "definitely the last obtainable, not to be repeated".

In 1944, to celebrate 100 years of the Co-operative Movement, concerts, whist and domino drives and dances were organised, and members of the Longridge Society received a centenary bonus dividend voucher of 3d. in the £. This heralded a period of rapid expansion by Longridge Co-op. At the beginning of the year, a new Grocery Order Dept. was opened at 1 Irwell Street, and shop premises at 28 Berry Lane were bought for future development. Further purchases followed: in 1945, of land adjoining the Grocery and Butchery Depts., and in 1946, of a valuable site in Grimsargh, at the corner of Longridge Road and Whittingham Lane, with sufficient area and frontage for two shops, and of the old-established branch of Messrs. Topping Bros. (Chemists) at 46 Berry Lane.

Monday, 14 October 1946 saw the opening of a Fish and Fruit Shop at 22 Berry Lane, and in the following year the sale of wet and dried fish was introduced at the Stone Bridge and Ribchester Butchery branches.

At the end of the War, five ex-army ambulances were bought, a coachbuilder was engaged, and they were converted into travelling shops to supply groceries to country districts. This was in keeping with the social conscience of the movement as they were never profitable, though they remained in service until 1982.

In 1948, the Society bought Seed's confectionery business and premises at 97 Preston Road, and Sumner's grocery and confectionery business and premises at 44 Berry Lane, next to the Midland Bank, to consolidate its provision in Longridge as it approached the 75th. anniversary of its founding. Its success can be seen in figures from the decades of the 20th. century:

	Members	Sales	Capital	Dividend
1906	1,133	£34,363	£20,233	2s.6d.in £
1916	1,311	£37,786	£26,081	3s.0d.in £
1926	1,360	£41,237	£37,563	2s.0d.in £
1936	1,787	£37,785	£56,657	2s.3d.in £
1946	2,549	£63,058	£109,997	2s.0d.in £
1956	2,947	£150,226	£134,248	1s.4d.in £

The 1950s were, perhaps, the high point of the Society. The traditional industries which had provided most of the employment in the village were declining. There was no longer the demand for Longridge stone for the public buildings of Lancashire towns. The three remaining spinning and weaving mills closed between 1959 and 1964 - in 1925 the village had over 2,300 looms. More people travelled to work outside the village, and many used the shopping facilities of Preston's shops and markets.

In the early 1950s, joint discussions were held between the Co-operative Wholesale Society Ltd., the Scottish Co-operative Wholesale Society Ltd. and the Co-operative Productive Federation Ltd. on the subject of co-operative production, manufacturing and marketing, both wholesale and retail. Having received a report on the outcome of these discussions, and noted the changing national pattern in retail distribution, the annual Congress of the Co-operative Union, at its meeting in Edinburgh in 1955, resolved to establish an Independent Commission. Its remit was to propose how the Movement could secure the best advantage from its co-operative productive resources.

The Rt. Hon. Hugh Gaitskell was appointed Chairman of the Commission, with Anthony Crosland as its Secretary.

Its report in 1958 found that the Movement was fragmented with too many small Societies, and recommended the merger of the smaller Societies to create more efficient units. Very few mergers followed, since Societies cherished their independence. However, on the retirement of its General Manager in 1968, the Ribchester Society decided to transfer its engagements to Longridge.

In 1970, the Co-operative Wholesale Society Ltd. built a large Regional Warehouse in Shay Lane, off Preston Road, Longridge, and this was one of the factors which enabled Longridge Co-op. to retain its independence for so long.

In 1974, the Society celebrated its centenary with a dinner for all staff, partners and friends at the Civic Hall. By the late 1970s, a period of high inflation combined with very high interest rates had brought about many mergers between local Societies.

The Preston Society formed the Lancastria Society which later merged with United Co-operatives to form the largest independent Society in Britain.

```
        MENU                          TOAST LIST

   Florida Cocktail                       —

        —                              GRACE
                                   by Mr. R. W. Wright
 Cream of Vegetable Soup

        —                               —

                             HER MAJESTY THE QUEEN
   Roll and Butter               The Duke of Lancaster
                                 by The Vice-Chairman
        —                          Mr. F. Beardsworth

 Roast Turkey, Stuffing              —
 Chipolata   Game Chips
 Roast and New Potatoes    THE LONGRIDGE INDUSTRIAL CO-OPERATIVE SOCIETY
 Garden Peas   Carrots                   LTD.
                               by The President of the Society
        —                           Mr. S. Maidment

  Peach Gateaux            Response by Mr. Ron Williams, J.P.
                             Area Organiser, U.S.D.A.W.
        —
                                        —
    Coffee
                                   TOAST MASTER
                                  Mr. J. W. Waring
```

Programme for the Centenary Staff Dinner Dance March 1974

By this time, the Longridge Co-op. had begun the process of closing its Branch shops, and the number of employees had fallen from 96 to 46. The Society had been unable to make dividend payments and had adopted a policy of "instant dividend" which proved unpopular.

At a meeting of members held on 19 September 1983, it was proposed that the Longridge Society should merge with United Co-operatives Ltd., a move which was supported by all the trade unions concerned. The members then voted to support the merger, which took place officially on 29 October 1983. Mr. Peter Farley, the Secretary and General Manager, in an interview with the Longridge News, stated that "the merger will not mean any major change for the people of Longridge", and added that he hoped there would be some improvements which would be for the better. He was also quoted as saying, "I do not envisage any closures of Departments, or at this stage that there will be any job losses".

However, within a short time after the merger, massive changes took place. The shops in the Central block were closed early in 1985, along with the Bakery, followed by the Butchery, Pharmacy and Fuel Depts., leaving only the Grocery self-service shop and the adjacent Bank, though a Pharmacy was later opened below Stone Bridge. The "Handy Bank" dealt with all services including current accounts on behalf of the Co-op Bank, and itself closed later in 1985.

United Co-operatives Ltd. decided to develop the area around the Grocery Dept. in conjunction with Ribble Valley Borough Council. The Berry Lane Medical Centre was built on the Society's land, and a car park created to serve the Co-op., the Health Centre and the village in general.

The units in and behind the Central block were let to various businesses, though the cost of leases has meant that there have been a number of changes in the past few years. Early in 1999, the whole block was sold to a development company as part of a portfolio of properties, and at the time of writing its future is uncertain.

Co-operation began as an industrial system, self-governed, and organised for the mutual benefit of its members. The immediate plan of the 28 weavers who started the first distributive store in Rochdale was to subscribe £1 each for the purchase of foodstuffs, to open a shop and to divide the profits from sales in proportion to the amount of goods purchased by each member. This principle remained the vital and distinctive feature of the Co-operative Movement. As it developed into a major retailing force, its progressive social role led its premises to be a centre for culture, entertainment and leisure.

Until the building of the Civic Hall in Longridge, the Co-op. Hall provided the major public meeting place for the population of the village and surrounding districts. Many a relationship began at the Saturday night dance, or one of the more formal and long-established Balls. It would be fitting if the Co-op. building could serve the people of Longridge as a community resource into the new Millennium.

This article is dedicated to the memory of Flight Lieutenant Sidney Clayton DSO., DFC., DFM., who was employed in the Co-op General Office prior to World War II.

NOTES
1. SMITH, T. C. A History of Longridge and District. 1888. p.88
2. Preston : a Handbook to the 39th. Annual Co-operative Congress. Whitsuntide 1907. Compiled by the Handbook Committee. 1907. p.130.
3. POTTER, T. Longridge News. 19 March 1981. p.4.
4. Ibid. 26 March 1981. p.8

Other information from L.I.C.S. Quarterly and Half-Yearly Reports and Balance Sheets.

LEE HOUSE, CATHOLIC CHAPEL IN THORNLEY

Leo Warren

Lee House, the Catholic Chapel set back from the road to Chipping from Longridge is a very quiet corner in the township of Thornley. Originally it was a yeoman's traditional farmhouse dating from the XVI Century and over the years has had an interesting and at times a turbulent history.

In 1738 Thomas Eccles, a local farmer (see illustration left) founded the Catholic Mission and settled on it land at Lee House and elsewhere to be held in trust. The income from the land and from the farms was to finance the small Mission. The original trustees were Thomas Walmsley of Showley, gent, Thomas Eccles of Dilworth, shopkeeper and John Cottam of Knowle Green. Further provisions were that a member of the Franciscan Order of Friars was to live at Lee House and officiate at the chapel there and 'that all the church stuff for the priest and altar, and my book of Religion may be preserved at the Lee House, and that the priest be not absent more than one week in the month'.

At that time such arrangements were in fact contrary to the law, public chapels of 'Papists' being permitted only from 1791. However in practice these did exist, often being maintained as the domestic chapel of some local Catholic family. One such was to be found at Lower Hall, Samlesbury, where the Franciscans were also in charge. They served too at the chapel at White Hill over the fell and continued to do so when the White Hill Mission was moved to Hill Chapel. Lee House however, was not dependent on the continued support of a local family but was in fact an independent endowed Mission.

The links between the Franciscans and the area were long established. In August 1646, at the time of the Civil War, a Franciscan friar, Father John Woodcock was one of the three priests martyred at Lancaster. He had been arrested earlier in 1644 in the district of Bamber Bridge.

Just one hundred years later, at the time of the Jacobite Rising led by Bonnie Prince Charlie, the first priest at Lee House, Father Germanus Helme (or Holmes) found himself in great danger. He was a local man from Goosnargh and he served both at White Hill and Lee House and was obviously well known in the area. He had been ordained in 1735 after training abroad at the Franciscans' Friary in Douai. In the political crisis provoked by the Pretender's Rising, he was arrested and thrown into Lancaster Castle. The conditions there were very severe and after four months he died while still a prisoner, and was probably the last Catholic priest to suffer in such grim conditions. He was 35.

The crisis passed and soon another Franciscan, Father Joseph Clarke, came to Lee House. He died peacefully in 1750 and the Chipping Register records his burial there on January 3rd.

The little Mission[1] continued to grow slowly and in September 1784 when Bishop Matthew Gibson came to administer confirmation to 33 persons, the congregation included 120 communicants. However two major changes were to affect the prosperity of the enterprise begun by Thomas Eccles.

First, with the excesses of the French Revolution, English Colleges (and Convents) abroad where priests were trained faced an increasingly difficult situation.

Students, priests and nuns had to flee before the revolutionary armies as best they could and return to England. Hence St. Bonaventure's Friary in Douai where the friars were trained and professed had to be abandoned. These were very dangerous times and Catholic priests in France were in great peril. For example Father Pacificus Knight O.S.F. who later would come to Lee House, was chaplain to the English Poor Clares at Aire in Artois. He narrowly escaped the guillotine only because of the fall of Robespierre in 1794.

The abandoning of the Friary at Douai contributed to the decline in the numbers of Franciscans available and they had gradually to withdraw from missions. There was no permanent priest at Lee House from July 1817 to May 1820 when Father Knight appears briefly and the last Franciscan departed in 1826.

Rev. Francis Trappes, 1790-1871

The second great change was the arrival at Lee House of the Rev. Mr. Francis Trappes. He was a secular priest, not a member of a religious order but he had been much involved with the Jesuits at Preston and Stonyhurst. He arrived on October 17th 1827 to find things at Lee House to be in a bad way. For the previous year there had been no resident missioner and a priest from Alston Lane had ridden over to say Mass on Sundays and Holydays.

Mr. Trappes, as he was known, proved to be very able, energetic and active at Lee House. He greatly altered and improved the original house and he built, more or less at his own expense, the small new chapel. The plan was the familiar one with the priest's house at the east end of the chapel building. This itself was a modest structure with a hint in the windows of the Gothic Revival that in a few years would make buildings like Lee House appear old-fashioned. A grander version of Lee House can still be seen at St Mary's, Chipping. Mr. Trappes also established a school where in 1837 there were 100 pupils, and he laid out a small burial ground.

In his first years, then, Mr. Trappes transformed Lee House and the congregation grew to over 300 communicants. He had every reason therefore to be proud of his achievements. It was a tragedy that all this progress was nearly brought to nought by the bitter controversy that engulfed both the mission and its priest when in 1841 Bishop Brown, the newly appointed Vicar Apostolic of the Lancashire District, suspended Mr. Trappes.

The wills of Catholics or 'Popish Recusants' as they were called had long presented peculiar difficulties. If the person making a will left money or assets for religious purposes such as for the saying of Masses, the will's provisions could be declared void on the grounds that the money was intended to be used for what were deemed to be 'superstitious purposes' which were illegal. In such instances non-Catholic relatives could challenge a will if they were so minded.

The Lawyers' defence against that danger was for there to be drawn up in such cases **two** wills: the public will which left moneys to someone with no wishes expressed about their intended use, and a second secret will in favour of the same person in which the deceased's religious wishes could be communicated. That in effect regarded the beneficiary as a secret trustee responsible for carrying out the deceased person's instructions. Further difficulties emerged if disaffected relatives became aware of the secret trust because it was then open to them to try to establish that undue influence had been exerted over the deceased by the trustee. That if proved, invalidated the will.

It was into such a situation as this that Mr. Trappes allowed himself to be drawn as a third party. The dispute was the celebrated Heatley Will case. Mr. Trappes' over-confident manner and his apparently assertive style combined with a strong sense of justice in the face of 'authority' would inflame the situation which proved to be such a disaster for Lee House.

William Heatley was a wealthy Catholic landowner who owned Brindle Lodge near Hoghton where he was known as Squire Heatley. His generosity to Catholic Missions was well known and several of his relatives included priests. Further, he was a bachelor. There was great sadness when he died in July 1840. Ballads were published celebrating his memory and good deeds.

The storm broke when his niece, Mrs Catherine Eastwood, learnt that while Brindle Lodge had been left with some land to her, the bulk of her uncle's money had been left to his spiritual advisor and friend, the Rev. Mr. Thomas Sherburne, Missioner at the Catholic Chapel called 'The Willows', Kirkham. Mrs. Eastwood and her husband and Mrs. Middleton, another niece, determined to contest the will, claiming that undue influence had been exerted over the old Squire. The case went to the March Assizes at Liverpool in 1841, where a compromise was reached whereby the Eastwoods gained £6,000 and all claims to the personal estate at Brindle Lodge. The Eastwoods however, persisted and petitioned Bishop Brown on the subject of priests like Mr. Sherburne who, they claimed, were influencing as confessors their penitents as they drew up their wills. Further agitation followed and by 1844 the House of Commons was petitioned to look into this and similar cases. In due course, in 1851, the Select Committee on the Law of Mortmain produced its controversial Report.[2]

But what of Mr. Trappes and his involvement in this unhappy dispute in Brindle? He was suspected by Bishop Brown (wrongly) of being the author of a pamphlet which was very critical of how such matters as the Heatley will were handled by the Church authorities. Further, Bishop Brown resented very much and viewed it as disloyal that Mr. Trappes had advised one of the nieces on a Canon Law question when the Heatley will was challenged. In December 1841 Bishop Brown appointed as his 'Grand Vicar', the Rev. T Sherburne who was very strong willed.

Lee House Catholic Chapel in Thornley
(print from Smith's History of Chipping, page 161, c.1893)

By this appointment the Bishop showed his confidence in Mr. Sherburne and so took his side publicly. In this way personalities became another factor in the controversy surrounding his decision to suspend Mr. Trappes.

In 1843 the Bishop recognised that Trappes was not the author of the offending pamphlet and the suspension was lifted, but he resolutely refused to allow Trappes or any other priest to officiate at Lee House. In other words he invoked the ancient procedure of placing the Mission under an Interdict and it remained in force for years: the effects of the original suspension and the later Interdict were that Lee House had no active priest for 19 years - it was in effect closed. This was probably the last time that a bishop had imposed an Interdict in England. By this time Bishop Brown was recognised as 'something of a Martinet' who regarded those who chose to appeal to Rome against his decisions as rebels.

The dispute rumbled on during these years. Trappes appealed to the Papal Courts in Rome and he firmly resisted Bishop Brown's attempts to gain full control of the Mission and its property, and to override and extinguish the rights of the lay trustees. Mr. Trappes finally won his case and was given full possession of Lee House.

Lee House, Thornley
(a modern view to compare with 19th.c. print, above)

Although vindicated he did not return but eventually handed over the Mission to the English Benedictines.[3] Father George Alban Caldwell O.S.B. took up his duties in 1859. By that date Bishop Brown was dead: he had become the first Bishop of Liverpool when the Catholic dioceses were established in 1850. Happily Lee House did not fall in his diocese but lay in the diocese of Salford - but only just!

The Benedictines from Ampleforth Abbey continued to serve at Lee House until the time of the second war and three of the monks are buried in the small graveyard. By the time Father George Caldwell departed in 1868, the foundation stone of the school-chapel in the centre of Longridge had been laid on the eve of Whit-Sunday, 1867. This development of the new parish of St Wilfrid's had an obvious impact on the size of the congregation at Lee House which steadily declined.

The Altar in Lee House Chapel

In the more recent times priests of the diocese of Salford looked after this tiny mission, but people particularly still recall old Canon Frederick Gillett, a retired priest of the Lancaster diocese. He was at Lee House eleven years. When he died at Lee House on February 1st 1969 the Longridge News reported 'He was also very human and approachable to everyone he met, his walks around the parish were prompted by halts for a chat at the various farms he was passing and he was ready to talk to anyone at all from children to adults, and from farmer to local landowner'.

Canon Gillett's successor, after Fr T.C. Collinson was Fr. Neil Maloney, who had retired from the RAF after 22 years service as a chaplain. He loved the place and he claimed that he had from his sitting room one of the best views in England. There were great celebrations for his golden jubilee, but he was to be the last parish priest of Lee House and in the November 1989, after his death earlier in that year, Lee House ceased to be a separate parish. The closure was a sad occasion and recalled the controversies of Mr. Trappes' day but the circumstances and outcome were quite different.

Lee House with its tiny chapel survived to have a new role as a centre of Mission Awareness and Mass has continued to be said there from time to time. Father John Sullivan arrived in November 1989, and was a member of the St. James Mission Society of Boston having spent eleven years working in Bolivia. He left in 1998.

In January 1999 the property was put in the charge of Mr. Joseph E. Howson and his wife Rosalba - Brandim with their two sons. For several years they had worked as lay-missionaries in North East Brazil. With the Howsons as custodians Lee House still has to have a valuable role in the quite different circumstances of the late twentieth century. It continues to be a centre for Mission Awareness with particular emphasis on issues of Justice and Peace, the Salford Diocesan 'Covenant with the Poor'. The chapel, house and grounds are presently being used for parish retreats, CAFOD days, prayer groups, marriage encounters and deanery Masses.

In view of the controversies that afflicted Lee House in former times, its dedication to St William of York is certainly appropriate. William's election as Archbishop of York in 1140 was bitterly disputed and there were appeals to Rome on the question. There the opposition to William was led by St. Bernard no less. He was deposed by Pope Eugenius III but following the deaths in 1153 of Bernard, the Pope and his rival, Henry Murdac, he was restored to York in 1154, but then he suddenly died and some suspected he had been poisoned. In 1227 he was canonised. William was a nephew of the hapless King Stephen whose reign, 1135 - 1154, was famously described in the Peterborough Chronicle as nineteen long winters when Christ and his Saints slept. Much the same comment could be made of the unhappy events at Lee House seven hundred years later in the days of Mr. Trappes.

References

1. The Baptismal Register dates from 1752 and is printed up to 1841 in the Catholic Record Society Vol,36: 'Lancashire Registers VI', with historical notes by Richard Trappes-Lomax. Sometimes the spelling Lea House is used: old Catholic missions are usually referred to by a geographical name rather than by the dedication. Examples include Alston Lane, Newhouse and Hill Chapel.

2. The Report of the Select Committee on the Law of Mortmain (1851). See also 'The English Catholics 1850 - 1950' edited by George Andrew Beck, Burns Oates, 1950 p.72.

3. He died at Clitheroe 1871 having been ordained in c.1821.

LET'S HAVE A REAL GOOD TIME - POPULAR ENTERTAINMENT IN LONGRIDGE 1840-1920

P. Vickers

The people of Longridge in the mid-Nineteenth Century were certainly not denied music and merrymaking. From accounts in the Preston papers it is possible to form quite a vivid impression of the entertainments offered, in particular around the Whitsuntide period. There are many reports of the parades accompanied by bands of music on Club Days and on these occasions the dinners at the Wheatsheaf and the Red Lion, organised by the Friendly Societies such as "Old Brotherly Society" and the "Sunday School Sick Society", were often rounded off with choral celebrations as in 1844 when "in the evening, at the Red Lion, songs were sung and airs played by a band from Hurst Green".[1]

At nearby Goosnargh the Sick Society had been formed about the year 1784[2] and had paraded and met for a brotherly dinner as early as 1835, but it was not until the report of the celebrations of 1838 that Preston Pilot stated that "On this occasion there was an increased attraction a number of the Independent Order of Oddfellows intended making a procession 'in full uniform' headed by the Preston Promenade Band".[3]

In 1843-1844 there were unidentified 'bands of music' at Longridge on Whit Monday but in 1845 a band appeared that was to form a mainstay of musical excellence in the area from then until the present day, the Longridge Brass Band. When they paraded at Goosnargh for the Independent Order of Mechanics they were described as Longridge (New) Band.[4] This period was clearly a time of great activity in the embryonic brass band movement, for Garstang Temperance Brass Band and Catterall Amateur Brass Band played at the Garstang Whit Walks in 1839, St. Michael's Brass Band is first listed in 1846 and both Chipping Brass Band and Clitheroe Temperance Band in 1847.

Apart from the spectacle of the parades and the general merry making the big attraction would seem to have been the dancing.

Report of Whit Monday procession, Preston Chronicle, Sat 6 June 1846

Again we turn to the elegant reporting of activities at Goosnargh in the Preston Chronicle, "Dancing was the order of the afternoon and evening, and though the mystic mazes of the polka, the voluptuous whirling of the waltz and the more simple movements of the quadrille were not in great repute, the hearty reel, the merry jig and the romping country dance were all joined with a zest that is never equalled at the balls of royalty".[5]

We are told that it was the merry strains of the fiddle that were called into action and the votaries of the dance kept up their amusements until nearly midnight.[6]

When Norman Parker wrote "The Preston and Longridge Railway" in 1972, he implied that the Preston Chronicle contains the following description of the opening of the railway on May 1st 1840, "At 10 am gaily decorated horses were attached to two trains of specially constructed wagons which then set off for Longridge accompanied by one of the local bands".[7] Unfortunately he does not give a reference to this information and neither the Preston Chronicle nor the Preston Pilot, which are the only two local papers available for that period, said anything about bands in their reports of the opening published on the 2nd of May. Perhaps he confused it with the running of the first steam drawn passenger train in 1848 when there was indeed a band, that of the 49th Regiment who were stationed at Fulwood Barracks, and later in the day the scholars of St. Lawrence's paraded behind the school band to witness the starting of the steam engine.[8]

Whilst the purpose of this paper is to examine and report on the social events in the Longridge district, we can't ignore the influencing events that surrounded them. In 1859, the threat of an invasion by foreign forces caused the then Secretary of State for War, Jonathan Peel, to instruct Lord Lieutenants of all counties to form forces of volunteers.[9] Many of these forces had their own bands to aid in recruitment and drill and in the surrounding area many such bands were formed. It was during the period from 1868 until 1871 that Longridge Brass Band became The Longridge Rifle Corps Band.[10]

The late 1870s saw many innovations in the Longridge area and included in these were trends in popular entertainment which were encouraged by the new Vicar at St. Lawrence's, Reverend Cave-Brown-Cave. In 1878 he was largely responsible for the organisation of the first Longridge Flower Show in a field near to the station.[11]

Starting in 1879, he published a detailed account of church events which has proved invaluable. From these records we see that he organised rail excursions to destinations such as Windermere, when on 12th August 1878 some 452 people, including two children, made the journey. On the excursions the party was accompanied by 'the Band' which, together with the choir, enjoyed free travel in exchange for their services. On occasion the Rev. Cave-Brown-Cave bore the expense of the band, but just who the band were isn't clear, but in all probability it was the St. Lawrence's School Fife and Drum Band.[12]

He also formed a branch of the Church of England Temperance Society in the October of 1878, the membership of which, including the Band of Hope, numbered 192 and was able to attract some 500 to a Tea Party by October 1879.[12] Lastly he 'took over' the Longridge Brass Band, who like the Bramley Band before them presumably all signed the pledge, for in 1883 they had become the Temperance Band of St. Lawrence's Longridge.[13] Harry Clegg states that "About 1883 the Rev. Cave-Brown-Cave formed the Longridge St. Lawrence's Brass Band"[14] but whether he formed a new band or did, as I would suggest, 'took over' the existing brass band is far from clear. To back this suggestion it should be pointed out that in 1879, a short-lived Alston Lane Brass Band played at Longridge and Goosnargh at Whitsuntide. As Alston Lane is the site of the Roman Catholic Church of Our Lady and St Michael, it is possible that the members of this band were bandsmen from the Longridge Brass Band who didn't wish to play in what had become a Church of England Band or sign the pledge?

It was on the 24th of May 1879 that the foundation stone of the new Co-operative store in Berry Lane was laid and this again was to herald important changes to a great many leisure activities in Longridge.

The Longridge Industrial Co-operative Society was formed in 1874 and prospered so that by 1879 work was started on a new 'Central Store' in Berry Lane. At the stone-laying ceremony there was a procession with the Longridge Brass Band.[15] When the New Central Store and Hall were opened on Saturday the 17th July 1880 "the proceedings started with a tea party and concert". A summary of the report in the Preston Guardian at the time points out that for an estimated outlay of some £3,000 the Co-op had built, after only seven years' trading, an impressive building that was not only commodious but provided a very pleasing aspect. Apart from the expected trading facilities on the ground floor and spacious cellar storage, the first floor provided a board room, an office and a warehouse and a reading room, a recreation room and a mixing room. On the top floor there was a splendid public hall, capable of seating 700-800 persons with retiring and other rooms.

Addressing the 600 or so gathered the Chairman commented that as the population of the village had increased by 1,000 between 1861 and 1871 and by some anticipated 2,000 between 1871 and 1881, the room which might seem too large at present would not be so in the near future. He thought that the provision of Reading Rooms might provide a counter-attraction to the Public House. Membership of the Society was 483 at this time. A concert followed the formal ceremonies with Miss. Pollard and Mr. Hugh Kirk providing the vocals and Mr. E.M. Bleany presiding at the piano.[16] Afterwards the Longridge Brass Band played for dancing until 11 o'clock.

The month of August 1880 was crowded with community activity. There was the Annual treat given to members of the Savings Bank by the Longridge Industrial Co-operative Society. Members assembled at 2.30pm. at the Berry Lane Co-op and at 3pm marched in an orderly fashion behind Longridge Brass Band in uniform, the Fife and Drum Band bringing up the rear. Messrs. Harrison, the President of the Society, and Molineux, the Secretary, walked in front and there were banners proclaiming the benefit of thrift etc. At a field in Kestor Lane, which was part of Daniel Platt Farm, there was a picnic with buns and other refreshments, sports and dancing. Six members of the Longridge Brass Band won the tug-a-war.[17]

The following week there was a picnic on Tuesday the 10th for a number of students and senior scholars attending the Independent Chapel, Berry Lane. Starting at 8am. they drove by waggonette to the beautiful rural district of Whitewell where they arrived at 10am. After a picnic provided by Mrs. Seedey, well known for her picnics, there was a ramble through the forest to the lead mines at Stakes in Bowland. Home for 6pm: a happy day.[18] Later that week there was a cheap train trip to Liverpool leaving at 8am. Some 6-700 people joined the train and many travelled further by steamer to New Brighton. They were accompanied by the Longridge Fife and Drum Band.[19]

Mr. Bleaney was at this time a popular figure and, in January 1881 he played the piano at the annual Congregational Tea Party and General Meeting in the Girl's National School. On receiving a vote of thanks he replied that "since settling in the area he had always felt it a pleasure to contribute to the musical capability of the place and to help forward as much as he could musical knowledge, and he was glad to say he had been successful to a large degree".[20] Just what his role was in the musical education of the area isn't clear, but in a later report when he played for dancing at a Co-op Tea Party he was described as a "professor of music".[21]

On a Saturday evening early in the January of 1881 the Annual Co-op Tea Party, Concert and Ball was held at the Co-op Hall, something for all the family. There were 600 for tea and Mr. J. P. Whittle took the chair for the evening. In his address he congratulated the members and committee on the success of the Society. They had "provided for a want long felt in Longridge by building a large room and that they had a suite of rooms below, warm and comfortable and admirably adapted for reading rooms". In the following concert the Glee Party comprising of Messrs. Crossley, Bentley and Proctor sang 'Pia Finda', 'Old Thomas' Day'and 'A B C', Mr. Gudgeon sang 'The Old School Master' and 'Oh! Where's My Dolly Gone'. Miss Ingrham sang 'Joyous Light' and together with Mr. Gudgeon 'Very Suspicious'. The room was cleared for the Ball and the Longridge Brass Band under the leadership of Mr. W. Walmsley mounted the platform and played for dancing to a late hour.

Brass bands were not of course the only purveyors of dance music. From the early 1830s at least a number of Quadrille Bands had performed for the citizens of nearby Preston as they held an annual series of Balls: The Ladies' Charity Ball, The Horse Fair Ball and the Catholic Ball to name just three. The members of the Catholic community in Longridge were quick to make use of the new facilities. Whilst a report on the first ball has not been forthcoming. the report on the Catholic Ball held on the 27th of December 1881 at the Co-op Hall contains a reference to a previous occasion. An efficient string band under the competent charge of Mr. Nelson of Preston was in attendance. Dancing was delayed until about nine o'clock when the strains of the band were heard and the ladies and gentlemen engaged in the first quadrille of the evening".[22] It would seem that the reels and country dances so popular at Goosnargh some forty years earlier were now abandoned as the citizens of Longridge sought to emulate the social patterns of the nobility.

Programme for St. Lawrence's Brass band 4th Annual Concert and Ball, Saturday 13th November 1886.

Mr. Nelson's band were again engaged to play for the ball of January 1883 and on that occasion "the band gave perfect satisfaction and the ball concluded between four and five on Wednesday morning".[23]

ANNUAL BAND CONCERT AND BALL.—The fourth annual concert and ball in connection with the St. Lawrence's Brass Band, Longridge, were held in the Co-operative Hall, Longridge, on Saturday evening. At the concert Mr. A. E. Ascroft presided, and Mr. J. Hindle officiated as accompanist. There was, as is usual on these occasions, a very large attendance.—In his opening remarks the Chairman pointed out the advantages that accrued from having a band in the village, and appealed to the inhabitants of Longridge to support the one they now possessed.—The band, which was under the conductorship of Mr. T. Sellers, then interpreted the polka (with cornet solo) "You can't resist" in a manner demonstrating skilful training. Miss Crossley sang very sweetly "Mother, bear me to the window," and, on receiving a well-merited encore, gave "Somebody's Coming." Mr. W. P. Bleasdale, Mr. J. Clegg, and Mr. W. Helm caused much merriment by their trio, "The Chimney Sweepers," for which they were rapturously recalled. Mr. J. W. Lloyd sang "Shipwrecked" in his accustomed able manner, and on being encored, gave "The maid of the mill." A laughable farce, entitled "Dr. Diaculum," was next given, the characters being sustained as follows:—Dr. Diaculum, Mr. W. Helm; Josh, his assistant, a curious chap, Mr. Jas. Clegg; Mr. Simpson, on business, Mr. W. P. Bleasdale; Police XX., on duty, Mr. Thos. Sellers. The band rendered the recitative and air (with trombone solo), "The death of Nelsou." Miss E. E. Clegg and Mr. W. P. Bleasdale followed with a comic duet—"Emily and John"—for which, on being deservedly recalled, they substituted another humorous duet, "The Naggletons." Mr. J. E. Smith was also encored for his skilful rendering of a comic song entitled, "The only one." Mr. Jas. Clegg recited "Uncle Dick's advice to wed women" finely, and a second appearance being demanded, gave another recitation, "The old bellman." Miss E. E. Clegg sang "The Stranger" in capital style, and in response to an encore gave "Farewell, ye lofty spires." The band came on next with a grand selection from "The Bohemian Girl."—Mr. E. S. Crook then proposed, and Mr. Sellers (bandmaster) seconded, a vote of thanks to the Chairman.—This was carried, and Mr. Ascroft having suitably responded, the concert concluded with a comic Lancashire sketch—"The Wedding at the Mill"—in which the respective parts were ably taken as follow:—Enoch Marsden, a millowner, Mr. Wm. Helm; Ralph, his brother, a scapegrace, Mr. Robert Clegg; Squelcher, a factory lad, Mr. Jas. Clegg; Sally, a Lancashire lass, Miss Jane Nuttall. The ball followed.

Report on the annual St. Lawrence's Brass Band Concert and Ball in Preston Guardian Saturday 20 November 1886

A typical string band of the period would vary in instrumentation depending on the size of the venue but some idea can be gained from that of Horabin's Quadrille Band who played in the Assembly Rooms at Preston in 1831. The Band comprised of two violins, a harp, clarinet, two horns, violoncello and double bass.[24]

The new halls were used, as intended, for lectures. Amongst those providing such were the St. Lawrence's Mutual Improvement Class. The Reading Rooms attracted 100 members by January 1882 but, proving that things don't change much over the years, "five young lads had been expelled".[25] Not everyone however used the new Co-op Halls, a Congregational Tea Party was held at the Girl's School in January 1883 followed by singing and a Magic Lantern Show presented by Mr. Clarkson.[26] The magic lantern was in its heyday in the late 1880s and "many organizations like churches and temperance societies staged regular lantern shows and owning a lantern for home use, with a toy lantern for the children, became a feature of middle-class life".[27]

Social activities continued much as before, but the annual Guild events due to be held in August 1888 were cancelled due to a small-pox epidemic in Preston, where many of the spectators came from. The outbreak was very serious and at its height sixteen deaths occurred in a twelve day period.[28] Not to be outdone the Sunday School and Day Teachers organised a picnic instead and some 170 teachers, scholars and friends set off in nine vehicles via Brock to Churchtown for refreshments and time to look around.[29]

The Co-op buildings were extended in October 1888 "to accommodate the Furnishing and Drapery Departments with a large room above for public use".[30] In the same month the Co-op Meeting, Tea Party, Concert and Ball attracted some 700 for tea and amongst the concert artistes was Mr. J. Clegg who was to become one of the central figures in providing entertainment".[31] Tom Smith writing at the time suggested that "There are two large lecture halls in the building, which will seat about 1,500 people".[32]

The Art of the Minstrel was brought to the shores of England by the Christy Troupe and the 'Ethiopian Serenaders' in the 1850s.[33] Whilst this form of entertainment is now regarded as distasteful by many people, this was not the case during the reign of Queen Victoria. The Empire was at its broadest and patriotism was at a level unimaginable in the 1990s. At the re-opening of Preston's Theatre in October 1880 the O.I.C.M. Minstrels appeared and in November of that year Matthew's Minstrels played for two nights at the Assembly Rooms. Not to be out-shone the Longridge Amateur Minstrels were formed and in 1888 performed at the newly enlarged Co-op Halls. "The first of a series of entertainments was given by the Longridge Amateur Minstrels at the Co-op Hall on Saturday. There was a large attendance. The first part of the programme consisted of selections by the whole company and songs by individual members. At intervals there were several 'black-faced' conversations in which many new and local jokes were introduced by Mr. J. W. Lloyd who was the Interlocutor together with Mr. J. Connell and W Prestwich who represented Mr. Bones. Mr. A. Dean played piano. The second part consisted of an original 'stamp speech' by Mr. J. E. Smith and a Musical Screaming Farce with J. E. Smith, J. Bamber, W. Prestwich, J. Lloyd and J. Blackburn".[34] The entertainment proved very popular and was repeated in late November in Goosnargh and in December in Chipping. Several months later the Ethiopia Minstrel Troupe performed at Mr. Broughton's Rooms in Grimsargh. These used to be adjacent to the old railway crossing and the advert in the Lancashire Daily Post on December 13th 1899 claimed that they had installed the 'Largest Electric Piano in England!'

The Co-op Hall was crowded for the Sixth Annual Ball organised by the Longridge Brass Band in December that year. Mr. H. Barker presided and in his remarks he referred to the fact that Longridge had greatly progressed as far as its musical notoriety went, and asked those present to support the band. There was a concert that included more minstrel humour and on the conclusion of the concert a ball was held, dancing to the strains of the band until after mid-night.[35]

Amongst the more unusual entertainments at this time was a concert at the Congregational School that featured, as well as the vocal contributions, dumb-bell exercises to music; an item that called for several encores![36]

Longridge Orchestral Band
2ⁿᵈ left Jack Clayton (?) euphonium, 3ʳᵈ left Fred Young flute and
leader (also played with Whittingham Band), 2ⁿᵈ right Cyril
Hothersall (?) violin, extreme right Jim Woodruff violin. Two
Coupe brothers also played with the Band.

As mentioned earlier the temperance movement took advantage of the latest technical innovations and so at the Band of Hope meeting held, again at the Congregational School Rooms, there was a magic lantern presentation of "dissolving views with powerful oxyhydrogen limelight".[37]

1899 saw the war clouds gathering as the Boer War began in South Africa but spirits remained high in Longridge. Mr. J. Clegg organised his second Annual Social Evening at the Co-op Hall in the January, it was well attended and Mr. James Turner's Orchestral Band played for dancing after the concert. Both these local men took up the stature of local celebrities in the following years. Also emerging at this time was the Longridge Orchestral Band who organised their second Orchestral Band Ball, which proved to be "not quite so busy as last year though an excellent programme of music had been arranged and dancing was kept up until the small hours".[38] Dancing was from 8pm. Gents 2/- and Ladies 1/6d. with a late bus leaving for Preston at 2am. The band was under the conductorship of Mr. James Turner but the advert on page one of the Preston Guardian for 4th February 1899 clearly states that this was the Longridge Orchestral Band Ball and this leaves quite a mystery, for Mr. Turner's Orchestra would seem to be a different organisation from The Longridge Orchestral Band. Unfortunately neither the descendants of Mr. Turner or other people interviewed have been able to throw any light on this association.

James Turner was born in Preston in 1862. He served his apprenticeship there as a draper and in 1885 opened a shop in Longridge. In 1905 he moved into larger premises in Berry Lane, opposite the Co-op Hall. His obituary in 1941 highlighted his many interests: playing water polo for Preston in his youth, breeding Borzoi wolfhounds and, of greater interest to our study, he played the violin and conducted a dance band in Longridge for some 17 years. Apart from these sparse facts no information has been forthcoming, but notices in the papers confirm that he led a band under his own name up to 1913, seemingly in parallel with the Longridge Orchestral Band.[39]

The Annual Concert and Ball was organised by the St Lawrence's Brass Band. The band was conducted by Mr. R. Rimmer of Southport and played a varied programme of music including a march 'Viva Pette', a selection from 'Zampa' and 'Recollections of Carl Rosa'. Following this they played for dancing until 11.30pm; "to wind up the very pleasant evening".[40]

In November 1899 three of the Longridge Reservists who had been called-up were given an enthusiastic send-off. "On Monday Lance Corporal Temple, Corporal Peter Robinson and Corporal John Kemp were transported in a landau trimmed with red, white and blue ribbons. The mill workers finished work twenty minutes early to see Sergeant Instructor Reeves lead the parade of reservists headed by St. Lawrence's Prize Band who played 'Rule Britannia' and 'The Girl I left Behind Me'.[41]

Early in December the Longridge Conservatives held their Tenth Annual Ball at the Co-op Hall and with Sergeant Instructor Reeves in charge of the decorations it is perhaps little wonder that these consisted of evergreens and Union Flags.[42]

A concert for the War Fund held at the Co-op Hall was a great success. A great programme of artistes were supported by selections played by the St. Lawrence's Prize Band. Stage decorations of flowers were by H. J. Lazenby and Mr. F.W.Dewhurst was the accompanist on piano.

Due to the serious fighting going on in the war the Preston Infirmary Ball was cancelled but the report in the Preston Guardian complimented the St. Lawrence's Prize Band in their efforts to provide something seasonal for Christmas which they did in a very successful social held in the Co-op Hall on Saturday last. After the concert dancing was kept up with spirit to the live strains of the band until a late hour. The duties of MCs were fulfilled by the Messrs. Parkinson. In a further effort to keep spirits high the band also played around the village on Christmas Day, in spite of the bad weather.[43]

As the Nineteenth Century came to a close we can see that the entertainment in the Longridge area, in particular the social dancing, had changed from being predominantly rural in nature to a more sophisticated pattern. The Court Balls of the late Eighteenth Century and early Nineteenth Century held in such places as Almack's Rooms in Bath, led on to the Assembly Room boom later in the century. The Corn Exchange in Preston had had the original three upstairs rooms made into one in 1848 and in 1882 a much larger room was built to the rear, in both cases to facilitate balls and suchlike. These were for the well-to-do and continued to be so in spite of a plea made as early as 1856 when a correspondent of the Preston Guardian suggested that a 'Working Man's Ball' should be held on the day following the Nightingale Ball, to make use of the decorations (it is presumed that 'working women' should also be included).[44] The important difference between the towns was that in Longridge it was the Co-operative Society that provided the public rooms which were made available to the whole of the population. They may have intended the large hall to be a lecture hall, but as we have seen it was only a matter of weeks before it was used for concerts and dancing. By early 1901 the war in South Africa had been resolved and the Victorian era ended with the death of the Queen in January of that year; the Edwardian era was about to begin.

The Recreation Hall Grimsargh re-opened for the season in October 1900 suggesting that its use was not continuous. The proprietor, Mr. J. C. Broughton, declaring that it was available for socials, weddings, birthday or funeral parties in addition to the dance classes and social on Saturday evenings.[45]

"Cinderella", 7 & 9 February 1914

Once again Longridge audiences were not left out of the enjoyment provided by developing technology; the Variety Entertainment provided by J. Bunce and Son's 'Sunny Vale Variety Company' of Brighouse, at Longridge Co-op Hall in March 1902 must have been quite an event for "the greater part of the programme consisted of a large number of really fine cinematographic films, exhibited on the latest 1901 and 1902 machines". They included a pantomime 'Cinderella', a trip to Sunny Vale, life-like reproductions of Little Tich, the Opening of Parliament and War Subjects. During the interval Professor Whittaker exhibited his skills as a ventriloquist and Madame De Ray gave some remarkable examples of Mind Reading.[46]

The Longridge Co-op Education Committee did use the Co-op Hall for its intended purpose and held a series of fortnightly debates. The subjects were "Dividend, uses and abuses", "Local Reforms", "The

Automatic Loom", "Competition v Co-operation" and "Friendly Societies".[47]

For the most part, however, the Co-op Hall was used for entertainment. In November Mr. Turner provided music at 'Clegg's Annual Social' and later in the month St Paul's Choir Social was held in the smaller Co-op Hall with music for dancing provided by F.A. Dewhurst, playing the piano, and J.H. Corbridge the violin. There was the Homing Society Prize Giving with musical entertainment and the Preston Guardian on the 15th November 1902 reported that "The Large Co-op Hall was crowded on Saturday last for a miscellaneous concert managed by Mr. E. H. Booth featuring the 'Japanese Opera Company' together with bird song and whistling by Mr. Derbyshire Winkley". They were closely followed by the Bentley's of Bradford Concert Party at the Co-op Annual Tea Party and Social when some 400 people sat down to tea.[48] Not to be outdone in the search for exotic entertainment a week later the St Wilfred's School had a concert with Mr. Horace Lingard's 'Japanese Serenaders'.[49] St Wilfred's was clearly quite keen to entertain and in December that year St Wilfred's Dramatic Society presented "A Convent Martyr" and 'A Rough Diamond'.

The Congregational Church had a concert. with Mr. J. Clegg and his humorous Lancashire sketches; Knowle Green Brass Band played a concert to raise money for a piano; the Longridge Brass Band held their Annual Social and to round off the year there was the Volunteer Prize Distribution by 'E Company' 5th Battalion Loyal North Lancashire Regiment at the Co-op Hall.[50] Clearly 1902 was a year with plenty of entertainment for the good people of Longridge with the facilities offered by the Co-operative Society playing an important part as a venue.

Whittingham Asylum had opened in 1873 and according to Albert. Clayton "At this time anyone who could play a musical instrument, or who happened to be a good cricketer, would be assured of employment at the Asylum". In his book 'Forgotten Fylde' there is a truly wonderful photograph of the thirty-five musicians who comprised the orchestra around 1906/7. Their musical offerings were not intended solely for those living at the hospital: in January 1907 the Lancashire Daily Post advertised the Whittingham Asylum Dance on Wednesday 2nd January with a bus to provide transport from Lune Street, Preston.[51]

Whilst Mr. Turner and the Longridge Brass Band, not forgetting Mr. F. Dewhurst and his piano, played at the Co-op Halls for socials, not all the dancing could be described as ballroom dancing. Not very far away from Longridge the Claughton Field Day was "to be held on Thursday 20th June in the same place as previous year; by kind permission of W. Fitzherbert-Brockholes. Chipping Brass and String Bands are engaged to play for dancing during the afternoon with a Country Dance at 7pm".[52]

In December 1907, there were balls organised by the Conservatives, the Co-op employees and of course the, by now traditional, socials to raise monies for the Longridge Brass Band. On Christmas Eve and the morning of Christmas Day the Longridge Prize Band and singers toured the streets.

1908 started brightly with neighbouring Dunsop Bridge having their annual ball, presumably in the school-rooms, to raise money for a reading room. There were some 160 people attending to dance to the Chipping String Band. It would seem to have proved popular, for the same report tells of a further dance with Messrs. Gudgeon and Bannister providing the music.[53] In the same week the Longridge Annual Farmers' Ball was held attended by some 400 patrons. The Co-op Halls were decorated with streamers and plants and Mr. Turner's Orchestra played.[53] Over 200 attended the Teachers' Social at Chipping, dancing until midnight to the music of Messrs. J.B. Corbridge and F.W. Dewhurst.[54] 'The Hot Pot and Dance' at Knowle Green organised by the Young Men's Club, had an element that was to cause much distress to musicians in the forthcoming years; they had a gramophone lent by Messrs. Watt Bros. of Longridge.[55]

The 28th Catholic Ball was held on Monday the 28th January at the Longridge Co-op Hall. The Halls were again decorated with streamers and plants and new dances were introduced by Mr. Turner's Orchestra. The mention of new dances prompts some enquiry into what dances were fashionable at this time.

Dancing classes had been available in the area, for those who could afford, since at. least 1811.[56] Clearly instruction must have been given in the Longridge area, for how else could dancing have continued, but it was not until December 1908 that mention of classes appeared in the newspapers. On that occasion dancing classes preceded the Saturday night dance at the Co-op Hall with Mr. Turner's Orchestra.

Longridge Prize Band, 23 July 1910, outside Woodville House, Longridge, the home of Band President, Fred Smith (hatless, centre).
> Prizes, left to right - Hawarden, Morecambe, Caernarvon (1908).Front Row left to right - Dan Fair, Jack Parkinson, Sam Wightman, ?, Jack Clayton, ?, ?, David Norcross, Tom Wilson.2nd. row left to right - ? Wilson (drummer), George Pye, Mark Sharples, ?, Fred Wightman, Fred Smith, Jack Wightman. 3rd row rt. Hary Clegg, Tom Walne, 4th row 2nd rt. George Wightman.

Victor Sylvester in "Modern Ballroom Dances" states that "at the beginning of the twentieth century the Waltz was supreme", although it had gone through many variations since the early eighteenth century. This is born out by the very detailed description of the Preston Infirmary Ball in the Preston Guardian of the 14th January 1899, where Mr. Sam Norwood's band played, mostly for waltzes.

Concert 𝔖aturday 𝔄fternoon, at 4 o'clock :: by the

LONGRIDGE PRIZE BAND

Conductor :   Mr. J. Clayton.

CONTEST MARCH ......" Harlequin " ....*Rimmer*
OVERTURE .... " Bohemian Girl " ....*Balfe*
GRAND SELECTION .....Weber's Works ....*Weber*
FANTASIA .... " Memories of the Past " ......*Rimmer*
LARGO .... Handel's Celebrated " Largo " ...*Handel*
SELECTION .... " Robin Hood " .... *McFarren*

*What harmony is this !
If music be the food of love, play on ;
Give me excess of it.—*SHAKESPEARE.

Programme for Longridge Prize Band at Longridge Congregational
Church Bazaar, 20-22 October 1910

What was to become a long established dance school in Preston, that of
G. Crooks, advertised that at his classes "the new promenade waltz
'Veleta' would be correctly taught," indicating a certain amount of
rivalry amongst his fellow instructors.[57]

Victor Sylvester includes the Lancers and Barn Dance amongst the
dances to be found on both the 'smart' dance programmes and those of
Country Balls and Private Subscription Dances and suggests that the
Quadrille and Polka were retained only for State Balls. It was a time of
great change on the dance floor and Mrs. Standring and Son of Latham
Street, Preston were offering instruction in the New American Cake
Walk in 1902, and by 1907 the American Two Step.[58] Just what impact
this had in Longridge is uncertain as no dance programmes from this era
have come to light but with the regular influx of dancers from Preston,
by bus and train, it is probable that the new dances were seen at the
Co-op Hall.

On the 8th February 1908 there was a report. on the Annual meeting of the Longridge Prize Band held in the band-room. It is worth noting this report in some detail as it tells much about how the band was organised. Funds at the beginning of the year had stood at £7-7-9d and the year concluded with an increase of £23-3-1d. The un-named President and Vice-President were re-elected. The following were also elected: - J. Clayton Bandmaster, J. Willan Assistant Bandmaster, T. Fare Treasurer, D. Pickup, Secretary, G. Isherwood, Assistant Secretary. The Honorary Members' Committee was to consist of H. Slater, T. Parkinson, J. Slater, T. Marshall, W. Emmett, G. Pye, J. Councell, J. Isherwood, J. Turner, D. Gardner, G. Wearing, and E. Seed. The General Committee was to comprise of J. T. Norcross, S. Wightman, J. Willan, J. Parkinson, T. Wilson, W. Wightman, G. Isherwood, J. Fidler. Auditors were to be H. Slater and D. Gardner.

There was a mixture of entertainment opportunities throughout the rest of 1908 with the now familiar dances and socials, a visit of the 'Ladybirds Concert Party' from Preston organised by St Paul's; a concert by the Knowle Green Brass Band in their school rooms, Mr. Turner's Orchestra played for the Longridge Amateur Dramatic Society, and a presentation by the Camera Club had animated photographs by Cyril Wilkinson of Manchester at the Co-op Hall, the evening's entertainment being concluded with mandolin solos from Mr. G. Marsh, accompanied by Mr. F.W. Dewhurst.

Towards the end of February there was a tea party social for members of the Independent Labour Party, formed in 1893. It attracted 60-90 for tea, dancing and the singing which included the "Red Flag". Not all the members were filled with optimism about a future in Longridge for in March there was a presentation from members of the Longridge Branch of the I.L.P. in the lesser Co-op Hall, to say goodbye to Mr. Morrow and family who were emigrating to Australia. Again, there was tea and dancing to Messrs. A. Ryding and W. Gudgeon.

In May 1910 King Edward died and the bands playing at Preston for the Whitsuntide walks were required to play only sacred music; they included Chipping Brass Band, Hurst Green Band, Ribchester Subscription Band and Knowle Green Brass Band amongst the thirty three bands in the Church of England procession. Longridge St. Lawrence, Prize Brass Band must have been elsewhere practising for on Whit Tuesday they won first prize at a competition at Hawarden, near Chester, beating Gossage's Soap Works Band and Foden's Wagon Works Band. In the same competition 1911, they won first prize in the quickstep section, second in the selection section and an individual medal for cornet playing. The familiar photograph taken outside Woodville House was published in the Preston Guardian in 1911. This was clearly not their first success as they had been referred to as Longridge Prize Band as early as December 1899. Later in 1911 they contested at Ullswater Sports and at the Winter Gardens, Morecambe they came second in the competition for a 50gn cup. The gold medal for cornet playing was won by Master Iddon Heap who was 13 at the time.

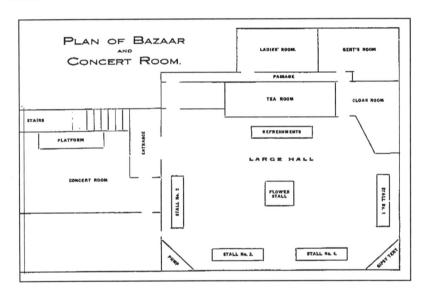

Of great significance to the social life in Longridge was the agreement made by the Urban District Council to take over the tenancy of Tootal Heights recreation grounds in December 1911. Again, laying the foundations of what was also to become an important part of the town's social life, it was in July 1911 that Mr. Clegg organised a social at the Co-op Hall with Mr. Turner's Band. By February 1912 we find that these evenings had become known as "Clegg's Long Nights".

John Cotterall in his publication "Preston's Palaces of Pleasure" tells something of the story of the Longridge Picture Palace. His statement that it was open for films in 1912 is borne out by the report of the concert in December that year held in aid of Longridge Brass Band that included a special exhibition of animated pictures. The Palace was still used for dramatic presentations, in February 1914 Longridge Amateurs presented 'Twelfth Night', repeated in March with funds raised being divided between the Lad's Brigade and the fund for the new Drill Hall.

In February Miss Alston, the head teacher of the Church of England Infants School, organised a production of the operetta "Cinderella" which was given at the Co-op Hall and raised £16 for the school fund.

With the threat of War again on the horizon, the Territorials gained importance in the life of the town. A new Drill Hall was planned and there was a parade of Territorials through the streets in May 1914 led by the Band of the Preston Territorials.

Longridge Prize Band at Tootal Heights Park

Later that month the Longridge Territorials held a dance at the Co-op Halls with the Longridge Orchestral Band playing for dancing. Socially little changed during the immediate pre-war period, Longridge Brass Band played frequently at the new recreation ground, Tootal Heights. Co-op employees enjoyed a trip to the C.W.S. Works at Trafford and some 2,000 people attended the Co-op Gala held in a field adjacent to the Stone Bridge.

When War was declared early in August 1914 the pattern of social life changed, but only in the sense that the social events raised funds for a new set of causes. In September the Co-op Halls were used for a recruiting meeting and in October Longridge Brass Band and others performed there in a War Relief Fund concert.

At Grimsargh Assembly Rooms a concert for the Belgian Relief Fund was well attended; two Belgian families were accommodated in Fisher's Square and one of the first casualties, Private Mason of the 1st Battalion Loyal North Lancashire Regiment returned home wounded.

Longridge Territorials' prize distribution, 16 December 1912

In spite of the unsettled conditions, dancing and socials continued with revenues raised going to the various funds for war relief. Mr. Fletcher allowed the Palace to be used for a general concert and Bioscope show with monies going to the "Queen Mary Sock Fund". 500 people, including twelve Belgians, attended the Annual Co-op Society Tea. Clegg's Long Nights came to the fore and as a result in December it was possible to purchase 25lbs of tobacco and 9,000 cigarettes from

Mr. Riley's tobacconists to send to the men of the Loyal North Lancashire Regiment.

Able men were urged to join the armed forces, and recruiting meetings were held throughout the rest of 1914 and on into 1915. In May that year Lord Derby arranged for the Band of The Liverpool Scottish to play at Tootal Heights, and in September the Harry Lauder Pipe Band added their encouragement. Over 100 men volunteered before the end of 1915. The Longridge Brass Band played volunteers to the railway station in view of large crowds of well-wishers. In June 1915 a Memorial Service was held to remember those Territorials who were never to return, The Church Lad's Brigade bugles played the Last Post.

Fancy Dress Ball, 14 January 1920

As the War continued so did the efforts of the fund raisers and at the events organised the people of Longridge were perhaps able to forget the troubled times they were living through. Clegg's Long Nights continued through to the end of 1918 dispatching well over £400 of cigarettes, tobacco and chocolate bars to the troops, whilst the busy knitters of the town produced 283 pairs of socks, 259 scarves, 34 woollen shirts, 24 mufflers and 69 helmets between July and December 1917.

Throughout the wartime period the prominent bands were the Longridge Orchestral Band and The Longridge Brass Band, who frequently played for dancing in addition to their contesting and parading. Dances and socials were arranged by many different organisations, more often than not at the Co-op Halls. Mr. Clegg and others, continued to organise socials after the War using these bands, and concerts at Tootal Height resumed in a more peaceful atmosphere.

In the Preston Guardian on the 15th November 1919 there was a report of the "Soldiers' Welcome Home" at the Co-op Hall where every serviceman was invited, by card, to attend with a lady friend. Over 1,000 attended with two sittings for tea. There was an impromptu concert by the Clegg Brothers and C. Rhodes, followed by a more formal concert and a ball when the Longridge Brass Band played for dancing. On the following Monday the committee entertained 700 children of the ex-servicemen for tea.

Children's Carnival, May 1920

Perhaps a fitting event with which to finish our look into Longridge in days gone by, would be the Children's Carnival organised in May 1920 by the Longridge Branch of the Fylde Division Women's Constitutional Association. The Preston Guardian reported that "The Hall was prettily decorated with flags, festoons and streamers when the event commenced with the dancing of the Polka, to a medley of 'John Peel". In all about 300 children of all denominations from Longridge and the surrounding districts took part, every boy and girl being attired in a fancy costume". After dancing the Valeta and the Barn Dance the next item was the crowning of the May Queen, Olive Riding, who was crowned by Mrs. James Openshaw. There were parades and prizes for fancy dress and more dancing. During the final balloon dance some 300 balloons were released. The children were provided with an excellent tea and a packet of chocolate. The Fancy Dress Ball in the evening attracted some 500 people who danced to the music of the Longridge Orchestral Band, once more there were fancy dress competitions and to complete the event Mr. Clegg supplied a liberal amount of ice cream.

Notes

1. Preston Chronicle 1st June 1844, page 2.
2. Preston Chronicle 6th June 1846, page 5, 62nd Anniversary of Society.
3. Preston Pilot 9th June 1838, page 3.
4. Preston Chronicle 17th May 1845, page 3.
5. Preston Chronicle 29th May 1847, page 5.
6. Preston Chronicle 1 st June 1844, page 3.
7. Norman Parker "The Preston and Longridge Railway", Oakwood Press 1972, page 8.
8. Preston Pilot 17th June 1848 and Preston Guardian 17th June 1848.
9. T. Herbert "Bands", O.U. Press 1991, page 25.
10. Preston Chronicle 6th June 1868.
11. Tom C. Smith "A History of Longridge" 1888, pages 71-72.
12. St. Lawrence's Accounts Report up to 30th April 1879 (Lancashire Record Office)
13. Preston Guardian 16th May 1883, page 6. Loyal Orange Procession.
14. Longridge News and Advertiser 11th October 1968.
15. Preston Guardian 28th May 1879, page 8.
16. Preston Guardian 21st July 1880, page 6.
17. Preston Guardian 7th August 1880, page 7.
18. Preston Guardian 14th August 1880, page 7.
19. Preston Guardian 15th January 1881, page 6.
20. Preston Guardian 8th February 1882, page 7.
21. Preston Guardian 18th January 188 1, page 7.
22. Preston Guardian 31st December 1881, page 7.
23. Preston Guardian 27th January 1883, page 7.
24. Preston Pilot 24th December 183 1, page 1.
25. Preston Guardian 7th January 1882, page 7.
26. Preston Guardian 3rd January 1883.

27. S. Humphries "Victorian Britain Through the Magic Lantern", Sidgwick and Jackson 1989.
28. T. Farrel, Lancashire Evening Post, 6th August 1992.
29. Preston Guardian 1st August 1888, page 7.
30. Preston Chronicle 13th October 1888, page 6.
31. Preston Chronicle 13th October 1888, page 5.
32. Tom C. Smith "A History of Longridge" 1888, page 89.
33. D. Paskman "Gentlemen Be Seated", Clarkson N Potter, New York, 1976, page 14.
34. Preston Chronicle 3rd November 1888, page 6.
35. Preston Chronicle 8th December 1888, page 5.
36. Preston Guardian 16th November 1889, page 3.
37. Preston Guardian 12th December 1888, page 7.
38. Preston Guardian 18th February 1889, page 10.
39. Preston Guardian 8th March 1941, page 6; Funeral of Mr. James Turner and also press cuttings from Mrs. Teasdale who is Mr. James Turner's grand-daughter.
40. Preston Guardian 16th September 1899, page 10.
41. Preston Guardian 25th November 1899, page 11. The names Temple and Kemp are unfortunately distorted in the newspaper and may not be quite right.
42. Preston Guardian 9th December 1899, page 10.
43. Preston Guardian 30th December 1899, page 10.
44. Preston Guardian 3rd May 1856, page 6.
45. Preston Guardian 15th October 1900.
46. Preston Guardian 15th March 1902, page 10.
47. Preston Guardian 11th October-20th December 1902, page 10.
48. Preston Guardian 22nd November 1902, page 10.
49. Preston Guardian 29th November 1902, page 10.
50. Preston Guardian 20th December 1902, page 10.
51. Lancashire Daily Post 2nd January 1907.
52. Lancashire Daily Post 13th June 1907.
53. Preston Guardian 8th January 1918, page 14.
54. Preston Guardian 1st February 1908, page 14.
55. Preston Guardian lst February 1908, page 14.
56. Preston Journal 7th September 1811. "Dancing, Mr. Robinson of Liverpool will give instruction to gentlemen prior to the winter amusements; Bull Inn".
57. Lancashire Daily Post 29th October 1902.
58. Lancashire Daily Post 19th November 1902 and 1st January 1907.

LONGRIDGE IN WORLD WAR TWO

John Earnshaw

When the Second World War started in 1939 Longridge was a self-contained mill village with a population of 4000. It had three working cotton mills, two foundries and two stone quarries. It was surrounded by farms and there were provender stores, blacksmiths and a slaughterhouse to cater for these. Local shops, especially the Co-op, provided for all needs – from made to measure suits and furniture to shoes and groceries.

One of the three mills, Queen's Mill, and the railway line to Preston
south of Stone Bridge
Before the war Queen's Mill wove high quality cloth for dresses
and curtains. The site and some of the buildings are now (1999)
used by Jones Stroud Insulations.

During the war Longridge was far from the front line. It was not even bombed. The war nevertheless had a major impact. Many, mainly the men, left Longridge for several years to serve in the armed forces. The others, mainly women, older men and children, waited anxiously at home for news of loved ones and meanwhile served themselves on "the home front". The anxiety, strain and shortages lasted 6 years and had a cumulative effect. It is easy to forget that for several years there was real uncertainty about the outcome of the war. For many people the war years were the most dramatic and eventful period of their lives. For some they brought injury, suffering or even death. For others they brought excitement and travel. For everyone they brought change.

It is hoped that this brief account of the impact of the war on Longridge will both stir memories and give younger people an insight into what life was like for Longridge people between 1939 and 1945.

The storm clouds gather

In the late 1930's many Longridge people read the "Preston Guardian". It is clear from back copies of this that it was a period of growing unease. The speeches of "Herr Hitler" were reported at length and studied anxiously as people considered the implications of his words and actions. In 1938 they learned of his march into Austria and of his annexation of part of Czechoslovakia. News was also filtering through of his treatment of Jews. Longridge men read that "Britain is moving towards National Service". Chamberlain's concessions in Munich were greeted with relief. However, by March 1939 a sense of crisis pervaded Europe. Everyone listened anxiously to the wireless for further news.

On Sunday 3 September 1939 the morning service in St Paul's church was interrupted by the news that war had been declared.

Death and destruction from the air

There was particular fear of attack from the air. Before long Longridge folk saw German planes on their way to bomb Liverpool and Manchester.

They saw the searchlight batteries trying to pick them out; heard the Ack Ack batteries trying to bring them down; and could see the sky over Liverpool and Manchester lit up by flames.

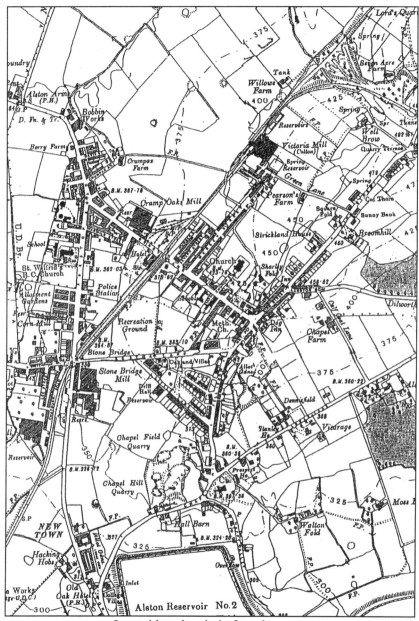

Longridge shortly before the war.
This Ordnance Survey map illustrates the importance of the mills
and the railway when the war started.

Friends and relatives gave graphic accounts of the death and destruction suffered. Even though no bombs fell on Longridge itself in the event – the nearest were stray ones in Grimsargh and Whittingham – the threat was real throughout the war years. There was a particular fear of gas after the horrors in the trenches in the First World War and even babies had their own gas masks.

Air Raid Precautions

As early as 1937 the Government required all local authorities to prepare and submit an Air Raid Precaution Scheme.

By the end of 1938 Longridge U.D.C. had established an Air Raid Precautions (ARP) Committee; agreed to purchase ARP handbooks and Ordnance Survey maps; appointed an ARP "Controller"; and the training of ARP volunteers, (including anti gas training) was well under way. This was largely by the police initially, with St John's Ambulance providing first aid classes. Rooms for these were rented in the R. Smith School (now Berry Lane C.E. Primary School) and in the Co-op.

In May 1939 92 badges were presented to ARP volunteers (60 men, 32 women) who had passed their gas and first aid courses

By the end of August the log book of the R Smith (Berry Lane) School was recording that "Lady Wardens (ARP) adjusting children's gas masks today" and the following month the U.D.C. appointed 4 men full time for "Rescue ARP work".

ARP posts were established at various points in the village e.g. in the basement of a cottage in Swarbrick Court on the lower side of the Dog Inn, at the bottom of Kestor Lane, and in a hut behind what is now Potters Motor supplies on Derby Road. The headquarters were in Towneley Road in an underground concrete bunker between what is now the Youth Club in Berry Lane and the British Legion Club at the rear. This was designed to house rescue parties, demolition squads and a gas decontamination centre.

Throughout the war years the ARP Wardens continued to undertake training; to man the sandbagged ARP posts; to inspect and advise on the repair of gas masks; to undertake exercises; and to patrol. At first they wore boiler suits. Later they were equipped with blue battle dress and beret.

The country had been plunged into darkness on the outbreak of war as an air-raid precaution and on their nightly patrols the ARP Wardens made sure all windows were thoroughly blacked out (many were also taped to prevent shattering) so that there were no lights visible to enemy planes. They also ensured that the few cars about had masks on their headlights. These had narrow slits directing the light downwards. No doubt these activities were an irritant to some, but for many others the knowledge that men were on patrol all night must have been reassuring. They and the firewatchers were also ready to put out fires caused by incendiary bombs with stirrup pumps and buckets of sand.

There were lighter moments. In July 1941 for example there was a novel bowls match between ARP headquarters and local wardens in which everyone had to wear gas masks and helmets. If removed the player lost 2 points.

The ARP Wardens also tried to ensure everyone went to a suitable air raid shelter when the siren went. The U.D.C. was authorised to build up to

ARP wardens playing bowls wearing gas masks and helmets July 1941

8 public shelters around the village each housing 50 people. One was sited at the top of Dilworth Lane and others near the Towneley Arms and in Kestor Lane adjoining Stonebridge Mill. These had a 9-inch concrete roof and 18-inch brick walls. The schools too had their shelters. Most people also had a shelter at home – sometimes shared with neighbours. Some of them were constructed of brick and concrete.

Most, however, were either 'Anderson shelters' – curved galvanised steel sections bolted together, partially sunk in the garden and covered with earth, or later 'Morrison shelters'- steel boxes put in a downstairs room and usually covered with a fringed tablecloth. Other uniformed services were also developed and expanded in preparation for the expected air raids.

One of the first was the fire brigade. In 1939 the U.D.C. authorised the purchase of premises at the Berry Lane/Towneley Rd junction to house a fire appliance and appointed an Officer-in-Charge to run the "Auxiliary Fire Service" (AFS).

By December 1940 there were 2 full time firemen and the "Commandant of Longridge AFS" was ordering 12 uniforms. In the summer of 1941 the unit and the premises in Berry Lane were taken over and became part of the National Fire Service.

The police service was also expanded by recruiting "Special Constables" to help deal with any emergency situation which might arise. The Women's Voluntary Service (WVS) was formed in 1938 and amongst many other activities constructed a field kitchen behind the Guide Hut in Irwell Street in case Longridge homes were bombed.

The Civil Defence Service was developed to organise local control should bombing or invasion seriously disrupt the normal pattern of life. The local leader would then have powers to co-ordinate rescue work and medical facilities and make the best use of the fire and police services, transport etc. Both the Civil Defence and ARP Services organised numerous exercises, usually on Saturday afternoon or Sunday and often utilising the disused quarries. They frequently involved the co-ordination of several services. The theme was usually a bombing raid causing building damage, people trapped and casualties. To test the capacity of the various services some "German" raids were very heavy, e.g. in one, 3 mills were hit, streets in the town centre were badly damaged, many people were trapped and buildings were on fire. This is the sort of thing which was already happening elsewhere, and there was a real possibility that it might happen in Longridge. In another exercise in May 1941 more than 20 casualties were rescued from an upper floor using lifelines and stretchers and people trapped in blocked air raid shelters were released via hatches.

Caring for the "wounded"
Participants in a joint services exercise in 1940 inside the Civil Defence H.Q.

These exercises were not without their humorous moments. Often a card was placed on the "casualties" indicating their injuries. At the end of one exercise St John's Ambulance personnel arrived late in the day to find the injured person had departed leaving an addition to his card which read "Bled to death. Gone home".

The Royal Observer Corps had the rather separate, specialist role of identifying aircraft by their outlines and, after dark or in a mist, by engine sound. Their base was on a mound near what is now Heathcote's Restaurant. It is thought that the Luftwaffe used the reflection of the moon from the seven reservoirs of Longridge as a navigation aid and that this made the role of the Longridge branch of the Royal Observer Corps particularly important.

The Services in Action
Several services are represented including the A.R.P., St. John
Ambulance and Longridge U.D.C. Note in particular those
responsible for gas decontamination in their gas capes

The Threat of Invasion & The Home Guard

In the early months of the war Germany conquered Poland, Holland,
Belgium, France and Norway in a series of lightning attacks. It looked
as if Britain would be next. The British Army escaped at Dunkirk but
was forced to leave its equipment behind.

An exceptional snowstorm completely isolated Longridge for several
days during the first winter of the war and this added to the anxieties of
the community.

Churchill rallied the nation with his "We'll fight them on the beaches"
speech. The response in Longridge as elsewhere included the removal
of all signposts, so that if parachutists landed they wouldn't know

where they were. This extended to shop signs such as Longridge Co-op and to school signs such as that at Thornley School.

The other immediate response was the formation of the Local Defence Volunteers (LDV). The volunteers enrolled at the police station on Derby Road. They were given LDV armbands but no guns. There was a particular fear that the Germans would make extensive use of parachutists in the invasion of Britain as they had in Holland. Members of the LDV were therefore sent on patrol above the reservoirs on Longridge Fell and told to watch out for parachutists on the Fylde plain. If they saw any the fittest was to run down to Longridge to sound the alarm!

The date stone and coat of arms from the old Drill Hall
This can now be seen alongside the War Memorial in Berry Lane

The LDV quickly developed into the Home Guard. Initially this included men of all ages, but as the war continued many of the younger men went off to serve in the armed forces. This left those such as farm and foundry workers who were in "reserved occupations" and were not therefore called-up and older men.

Longridge was fortunate in that it had a Drill Hall on Little Lane which had been purpose built in 1914 for the Territorial Army. It included a hall, a shooting range, armoury, rest room, games room and offices. It formed an admirable base for the Home Guard and was used as both a battalion HQ and as the company H.Q. for platoons from Goosnargh and Grimsargh as well as those from Longridge itself.

The men -there were no women- were issued with uniforms, .303 rifles, tin hats and gas masks. Later they acquired mortars, 2 Vickers machine guns and Sten guns. Their training included map-reading, unarmed combat, rifle, Sten gun and mortar practice. Most of the training took place at the weekend, often in local quarries, but occasionally on the Rossall School shooting range near Fleetwood and elsewhere.

Each man had to be on duty one night a week. This was usually at the drill hall and if they were lucky they had a "kip" on a straw mattress for part of the night before they returned to work the following day. However, from time to time they also had to undertake guard duties at the bottom of Elston Lane where the water main from Thirlmere to Manchester crosses the river Ribble, and by the reservoirs.

The Home Guard also manned a roadblock on the road from Preston on the Longridge side of the Alston "White Bull". Anyone coming towards it was checked, including all bus passengers. In the case of double decked buses one sentry went upstairs and another down. Anyone who didn't have a satisfactory Identity Card was taken to the police station.

The Pillbox guarding the entrance to Longridge

Now (1999) obscured by vegetation, but still just visible on the road to Preston opposite the end of Alston Lane.

The roadblock and Pillbox were near the line of an anti tank ditch dug by the army from Woodplumpton to Ribchester. The Pillbox is still there (1999) albeit hidden by vegetation.

Manoeuvres and exercises were a regular part of the training. On one, the mission was to evade the Blackburn Home Guard and reach Blackburn Town Hall. They succeeded by commandeering the Blackburn police inspector's car at gunpoint and using this as cover for the last part of the journey.

Life in the Armed Forces

Before the war most Longridge people had always lived in and around Longridge. Few indeed had been abroad. In contrast during the war a high proportion of Longridge men between the ages of 18 and 40 served in the armed forces and, as a result, travelled widely for several years. They joined the army, the navy and the air force; they served in the artillery and the infantry; in minesweepers and in battleships; in bombers and in fighters – and they did so in all corners of the globe from Canada to North Africa, from Burma to Singapore and from Italy to France and Germany.

When the war started a few reservists were "called up" at once. For most young men, however, there was a period of uncertainty. Some volunteered (essential if they wanted to fly), others waited for their age group to be called for medical examination. This took place in Preston. There was then a further period of waiting before they were "called up" to start their training.

As the war continued the age group conscripted widened and the number of occupations which were exempt from war service diminished. More and more men therefore left Longridge as the war progressed.

The experience of each was unique. One example from each of the services must suffice by way of illustration, but none can be regarded as "typical". They are anonymous, as it would be invidious to pick any out any one serviceman for special mention.

One man found himself in a "reserved occupation" at the beginning of the war because his mill had turned over to making cloth for the services. However, he saw more and more of his contemporaries being called up and knew his turn would come. When it did he asked to be posted to R.A.M.C. because of his first aid experience in the ARP, but found himself in the Royal Artillery instead. After training at various places in England he was sent to join a convoy in Glasgow. He had no idea where they were going. In fact they went via the Atlantic, Capetown, and the East Coast of Africa (and several U-boat attacks) to the Suez Canal. There he joined the 8th Army – the Desert Rats- as they fought their way across N. Africa (sandstorms were a major problem) and thence to Sicily and up the whole length of Italy to the Po Valley in the North. On the way he earned a Military Medal for outstanding service.

Another man, who was only 16 when the war started, volunteered for the airforce in the hope of qualifying for aircrew. After assessment he resumed work until he was called up in 1941. He had to travel to London, Leicester, Aberystwyth, Manchester and North Wales for various aspects of his training before joining a squadron of Lancaster bombers as a navigator. He then took part in 23 night raids over Germany. After every trip, those who had returned checked at breakfast the following day which crews were missing. Whilst he was in hospital after his 23rd trip his own crew were lost over Germany.

A third man who was in his mid 20s in 1939, registered for conscription like many "to do my bit" soon after war started. He was keen to join the Royal Navy and succeeded in doing so. His training took him to Skegness, Plymouth, Lowestoft and Edinburgh. He then joined an old paddle steamer which had been equipped with guns to defend the mouth of the Thames. After this he was transferred to a trawler which had been adapted for minesweeping along the East Coast. Having survived this (unlike others), he then went via a spell in Chatham to Freetown, Sierra Leone, a major staging post for the Royal Navy at that time. He was there when the war ended.

Several hundred Longridge men had comparable - if different experiences. A number, sadly, lost their lives or were wounded. Others had to endure long periods in Prisoner of War camps.

A few young women also served in the armed forces. One describes how, as a single young woman of 20, she was given the choice of going into the forces or into a munitions factory. She chose the forces. Life in barracks was a shock, but she enjoyed the drill and the training for work in an Anti-aircraft (Ack Ack) battery. The women manned the range and height finders and the telephones. She served in Anglesey, Glasgow, and Hampshire and ended the war in London at the height of the V1 and V2 rocket attacks. Despite this she enjoyed her time in the ATS, describing it as "exciting" – "it put you on your mettle".

The War Memorial in Berry Lane

The use of Longridge stone in this fittingly symbolises the strength and character of the Longridge men who served, and in some cases gave their lives, in the armed forces. The plaque reads,

"To the fallen; we will remember them".

The badges in the side walls are those of the Royal Navy, the Army, the RAF and the Merchant Navy.

One of the most striking features of the newspaper reports of the war years is the number of decorations awarded to Longridge men – surely more than average for a community of 4000. For example one pilot received the DFM, DFC and the DSO; an army officer was awarded the Military Cross while serving with the Chindits in Burma; a Chief Petty Officer, who was chief engineer on an armed trawler, was awarded the DSM; and there were many more.

War Work – New roles for women

In addition to the women who left Longridge to serve in the armed forces, a number of others went to fulfil vital support roles. One, for example, was in charge of a ward in a Casualty Clearing station which gave preliminary treatment to men rushed from the front line throughout the allies' advance from Normandy to Germany.

Most, however, undertook new roles in and around Longridge. In the mills more women were employed to replace the men who were called up. Many had to switch from weaving expensive shirting and fine dress fabrics to weaving such things as denim for the army. In all the mills employed about 600 people.

In the Belmont and Poplar Foundries, both on Inglewhite Road, the men were exempt from military service because they were engaged in vital war work, but extra workers were needed and women were recruited.

The Poplar foundry, (now Ryans) employed 125 people. It made large quantities of windlasses for barrage balloons, rope grips for submarine nets, capstans and smaller parts for ships such as ventilators and porthole covers, davit blocks for lifeboats and anchors.

The biggest change for women, however, came when they were recruited in large numbers for war work in the surrounding area e.g. 150 travelled by special buses each day to Courtaulds (situated where the Red Scar Industrial Estate is now) to make such things as parachute harnesses and tyre cords. Others travelled to Euxton R.O.F., which employed up to 35,000 people, mainly women, making munitions. They were easily identified by their stained skin, which was turned yellow by the sulphur used. Others went to English Electric (more recently British Aerospace) in Preston which turned out 3,000 Halifax and Hampden Bombers during the course of the war; and to Leyland where they were engaged in precision engineering work making tank parts. Much of this was shift work and hours were long to secure maximum production.

Women also undertook new roles on the farms as "land girls". The sinking of merchant ships by U-boats posed a major problem. It was vital to produce more food at home and to grow more animal feed.

Bringing in the Harvest
Friends and family helping to harvest oats on Lancaster Farm, Thornley, with Longridge Fell in the background. The Ministry of Agriculture compelled farmers to plough up some of their pastures and grow crops like oats in order to reduce dependence on imported animal feed.

The Ministry of Agriculture therefore required farmers around Longridge, often against their wishes, to plough up some of their pasture and plant crops such as oats, kale, swedes and potatoes. They were also encouraged to make silage to replace imported cattle cake. One slogan of the time was "Ploughing on Farms is as vital as Arms". Farm workers were exempt from military service but all this work required extra labour and women were recruited to the "Womens Land Army" to provide some of it. They were posted to where they were needed. One young girl who lived in Barrow-in-Furness was posted to a farm in Longridge. She thought the local farmers were a friendly lot. So friendly in fact that she married one and settled down in the area after the war.

Women also found new roles in voluntary work. Many joined the newly created Womens Voluntary Service. In the Guide Hut on Irwell Street they sewed clothes for the forces –pyjamas were apparently a local speciality- and rolled bandages; they also formed knitting groups and packed parcels of comforts for the troops; they raised funds and collected salvage. Longridge women also helped to staff the famous Preston Railway free buffet.

W.V.S. volunteers sewing clothes for the Forces and rolling bandages in the Guide Hut.

This provided much appreciated free refreshments for the many thousands of servicemen who passed through Preston by day and by night to new postings throughout the war years.

"Waste not Want not": Rationing, Salvage and Fund-raising

By the end of the war Britain had 5 million men in the armed forces. Large resources were needed to feed, clothe and equip them. At the same time many merchant ships were being sunk by U-boats and this reduced the quantities of food and raw materials which could be imported. Food and materials of all types were therefore in very short supply.

Part of the government's response was to introduce rationing. Food rationing started in January 1940 for bacon (weekly ration 4 ozs) butter (4 ozs) and sugar (12 ozs). Meat followed in March. In July the butter ration was halved and tea rationing introduced. Later most other types of food were also rationed. To supplement these meagre supplies everyone was urged to "Dig for Victory" – to grow food in their gardens and in allotments. In October 1939 the Longridge allotment campaign was launched in the Co-op Hall and in March 1942 the local press reported a "Dig for Victory" exhibition at the Central Saleroom. In December 1941 Longridge and District "Fur and Feather Club" held its first show. The aim was to raise rabbits and poultry for food. In August 1943 Longridge U.D.C. decided to give all fruit and vegetables "grown at the sewage works" to Preston Royal Infirmary!

Longridge was able to cope with food rationing better than many areas because it was surrounded by farms. Many people knew someone who kept hens or a pig or even milking cows and were able to supplement their diet. Longridge schoolchildren made voluntary collections of eggs for the Whittingham and Preston hospitals.

Many types of food we take for granted were almost totally missing e.g. ice cream, bananas and oranges. When a consignment of South African oranges did get through to Preston in September 1941 it merited a special report in the local paper. One Longridge man recalls that he managed to get 3 of the oranges for his girlfriend and reminded her of this several years later when he asked her to marry him.

Clothing too was rationed from 1941. Turn-ups were forbidden on men's trousers to save cloth. Later the "utility" standard was introduced for clothes and with it shorter skirts and a limit on how many buttons could be used on garment of various sorts. This was followed in 1943 with a "Make Do and Mend" campaign. Everything had to last longer. Again Longridge people coped better than most. There were after all three cotton weaving mills in the community and there are also stories of farmers wives who went to market in Preston and exchanged farm produce for clothes. The women making clothes for the armed forces in the Guide Hut were the grateful recipients of 100-yard rolls of material from a local draper, free of charge and no questions asked.

The shortages affected all aspects of life. Fuel was also in short supply. In 1939 the U.D.C. appointed a "Fuel Overseer" who had the invidious task of allocating supplies of coal reaching Longridge as fairly as he could. In December 1941 the local paper even carried a report that 1941 was to be the last year in which Christmas cards could be sent in order to save paper.

There was a great effort to make use of existing resources by collecting "salvage". The Longridge Salvage Stewards Committee was set up to

 co-ordinate the efforts of many groups. Throughout the war years there were special drives to collect paper, bones, tin, aluminium pans etc, clothing, rags and even string and gramophone records.

A reminder of the World War 2

The stumps of iron railings removed during the early years of the war still (1999) visible just below the junction between Berry Lane and Church Street.

One salvage drive is worthy of special note. In September 1941 the Ministry of Defence instructed the U.D.C. to let the Ministry have a list of "iron railings, gates, posts, chains, bollards and similar articles". These were later removed to be turned into armaments. The stumps of the wall railings are still visible in Berry Lane 60 years later just below the Church Street junction and elsewhere.

A related activity was the collection of rose hips and heather on Jeffrey Hill by school children. The rose hips were used to make rose hip syrup and the heather for camouflage at Samlesbury aerodrome.

The community also found the energy to organise numerous fund raising activities. These ranged from dances and whist drives to carol singing and from concerts to street and house collections. Among the more unusual methods was a "Penny a Peep" show which was organised when a German propaganda leaflet dropped by air found its way to Longridge. The proceeds from this and many other efforts went to the Forces Comfort Fund.

Other causes which benefited ranged from the Red Cross and the Preston Station free buffet fund to the Aid to Russia Fund. There were also special efforts to raise funds to contribute to the purchase of armaments e.g. in 1940 towards the cost of a squadron of Spitfires to be called the Lancastria Squadron, and in 1942 towards the cost of a tank to be called the "Preston". The drive for National Savings was always an important part of the war effort too. In 1943/44 Queen's Mill won the Lord Derby cup for the highest National Savings per head in the whole of the textile industry.

In December 1944 it was reported that "The War Office has presented savings plaques to Longridge due to the large amounts raised in War Weapons Week (1941) Warships Week (1942), Salute the Soldier (1944) Wings for Victory and others.

Many groups such as the W.V.S., the Churches, the Co-op, the Mills, the schools and others knitted socks, balaclavas and blanket squares, and prepared parcels of comforts for Longridge men serving in the armed forces.

The newspaper reports refer to these as containing both luxuries and necessities. It is clear, however, that ideas of what are luxuries must have changed when we read that the 1941 Christmas parcels from one typical organisation contained "socks, handkerchiefs, razor blades shaving soap, writing material and a postal order".

The Guide Hut was a particular focus. Several thousand garments were knitted and sewn, numerous bandages rolled and large numbers of parcels of "comforts" packed. The Red Cross collection boxes were also counted out there. The decision of the U.D.C. in October 1939 to rent it "for the duration of the war" for 7 shillings a week had proved a wise one.

The Guide Hut in Irwell Street

The centre of W.V.S.activity throughout the war years.

Transport was another shortage area nationally. The railways had to provide transport for large numbers of servicemen moving between training camps and postings, for raw materials and for finished munitions. The buses had to transport extra workers to the munitions factories and mills. At the same time there was a shortage of coal and supplies of fuel oil were reduced by shipping losses. People were therefore urged to travel as little as possible. One poster asked "Is your journey really necessary"?

A Longridge woman who travelled to teacher training college in Darlington between 1943 and 1945 found the mainline trains crowded with servicemen, dirty, smoky and dimly lit. The branch line from Preston to Longridge had ceased to run passenger trains in 1930, but during the war it carried two goods trains a day to bring in coal, iron, (cast and scrap), zinc and aluminium, moulding sand, spun cotton, rayon and wool and to take out ships fittings and cloth. Where the Towneley Parade of shops and parking area is now, was a bustling goods yard and Stonebridge Mill made full use of its siding. The Victoria Mill had been closed for 4 years when the war started but it was used by the Ministry of Defence to store rubber tyres and belting and on at least one occasion a trainload of explosives was parked in its siding.

The number of lorries available for local transport was depleted when two were sent to the South coast in response to a government appeal to replace lorries left behind at Dunkirk. Petrol rationing and the absence of signposts also made life difficult for local transport contractors. They had some unusual tasks. For example they carried several thousand tons of quarry waste from the "Tootle Heights" area currently occupied by the Caravan Park to Warton and Inskip to provide foundations for new airfield runways and hangers. They also retrieved cargoes from Liverpool e.g. on one occasion when a ship limped in and partially sank, they carried its cargo of damp wheat to the farms for use as pig feed. Another unusual task was carrying Italian POWs to work on the farms. The lorries were equipped with benches for the purpose with 18 inches allowed per prisoner.

Few people had cars then and severe petrol rationing made it difficult for those who did to use them. In 1942 even the meagre ration that had been allowed was abolished. Petrol thereafter was for industrial and commercial use only.

Most people relied on buses. Priority was given to getting people to work. In addition to the special buses provided to places like the Euxton munitions factory, workers were given priority over shoppers on the reduced number of ordinary buses e.g. Ribble Motor Services Ltd placed a notice in the paper in December 1942 advising "No Christmas Day buses. Buses will be as for mid-week days on Boxing Day from 10-00am. Services essential for work people will operate on both days". At one period some buses, including those to Clitheroe, ran on gas from a trailer they towed behind.

Many people recall that the last bus to Longridge from Preston, even on Saturdays, was at 8-15pm.

Strangers in Town

During the war years the Longridge community had to adjust to the absence of most of its young men. It also had to deal with the arrival of various groups of strangers.

The first of these to arrive were children from the Ancoats and Ardwick areas of Manchester and a few of their mothers. The government had planned a mass evacuation of children from the major cities well before the war started to safeguard them from air raids. They put these plans into action on September 1st 1939 in anticipation of the formal declaration of war. The first children sent to Longridge arrived in three double decker buses. They had with them their gas masks, a small case, and a packet of groceries provided by the authorities. They had their names on a label round their neck. They were taken to the Co-op Hall to be selected and collected by their hosts in what was clearly a traumatic experience for many of those concerned. In all nearly 500 mothers and children were billeted in the Longridge district. Some settled and enjoyed their new rural environment. Others were homesick. Most of the evacuees were R.C.s and half time schooling was therefore necessary at St Wilfreds. However, there were no air raids that autumn and many of the evacuees therefore started to drift back to their homes in Manchester. By Christmas almost all had gone and that particular group did not return.

Others came and went in their stead, however, as the Germans started to bomb London, Manchester, Liverpool and other cities heavily. Most came under official schemes. Others came in ones and twos to stay with relatives. In December 1940 it was reported that "the Guide Hut will be open every Wednesday afternoon as a meeting place for the London evacuees". In October 1941 Broomhill Lodge in Higher Road was opened as a hostel for evacuee boys from the surrounding areas who had health problems. The WVS played a key role in obtaining furniture and equipment for it.

Some of the evacuees were elderly Londoners evacuated from sheltered housing in Southwark. There were communication difficulties in view of the different accents, but some enjoyed the rural environment so much that they cried when it came time to return to London. Towards the end of the war the V bomb raids on London led to more evacuees coming to Longridge e.g. in August 1944, 12 mothers and 38 children arrived from London. "They were received at the Co-op Hall and given lunch and tea whilst accommodation was being settled". Another group who came to the Longridge area in the early days were the soldiers wounded in the Dunkirk evacuation. Several hundred came to Whittingham hospital for treatment and were seen around the area as they convalesced.

Later in the war Whittingham hospital also cared for wounded POW's. Some of the care was provided by displaced persons from countries like Estonia and Latvia which had been over run early in the war. Several of these settled down and remained in the area after the war. Other POW's were accommodated in Longridge itself. Alston Lodge on Lower Lane was used to house a large contingent of Italian POWs. These seem to have posed little threat. They were allowed to walk unescorted as far as St Lawrence's church and taken out daily without escort to work on surrounding farms. There are reports that their singing could be heard at the top of Dilworth Brow. This may be explained by the distilling stills for wine and beer which were found hidden in the loft when building work was undertaken in Alston Lodge after the war.

Alston Lodge as it is now (1999)
The lodge housed POWs during the war. Now it is a residential home for the elderly

When Italy made peace in 1944 the Italians were billeted on the farms and German P.O.W's took their place. Unlike the Italians the Germans were not allowed out unescorted. However the farmers regarded them as good workers and at least one settled down and remained in the area after the war.

No British Army units were billeted in Longridge itself but there were searchlight batteries at the bottom of Hothersall Lane in the area now occupied by the Field Study Centre, behind the Derby Arms in Thornley and on Cow Hill. The Army practised river crossing at Elston and Red Scar was used as a firing range. Longridge Show Field was used for a tented rest and recreation camp for bomb disposal units from Liverpool and troops on manoeuvres passed through from time to time. On occasions these were billeted in the Drill Hall, the Co-op and the Berry Lane school together with their bren-gun carriers and other equipment. For example the school log for 13 August 1943 records "Lancashire Fusiliers billeted in school tonight. Gate jamb damaged by army lorry".

Of even greater interest to local schoolboys, however, was the large army training ground between Saddle Fell and Parlick Fell near Chipping. There they could collect spent shells -and even live ones. They extracted cordite from the latter to make fireworks!

No Americans were billeted in Longridge itself either, but in the build up to D-Day a number of American camps were established nearby and their jeeps were often seen in the area.

Dances and Dominoes

As few people had cars and the last bus from Preston left at 8-15pm, entertainment had to be organised locally. The large hall above the Co-op was by far the most popular venue with dances every Saturday night and balls on many Wednesdays. These often attracted 500-600 people who danced the night away to the music of the "Masqueraders", the "Rhythm Aces" or the "Arcadians".

Dominoes were organised in the anteroom for the less energetic. There were many newspaper reports like the one in March 1943 stating that "An ARP dance, whist drive and domino social was held at the Co-op Hall last Wednesday. The Arcadians and the Rhythm Aces provided the music. There were 41 whist tables and 60 domino players".

Social gatherings were however, also held elsewhere. For example in August 1942: "A billiards, darts and dominoes match was held at the Dog Inn, ARP HQ versus Wardens. Supper was provided and funds raised for Preston Station Free Buffet".

An advert for a dance in the Coop Hall in August 1944

In February 1944: A domino drive and hot pot supper in the Guide Hut raised funds for "local sick and wounded servicemen presently in hospital".

The Palace cinema on Market Place was another popular entertainment centre with films shown every night and twice on Saturdays, although there was a report in April 1943 that "cinema shows are likely to become shorter owing to a shortage of celluloid".

Established sporting activities continued with older and younger players taking the places of those away. New ones were added such as the "Local Civil Defence Services Bowling League" which was established in 1941 with 2 ARP teams and others from the AFS and Whittle Mill.

Much of the entertainment was organised to raise funds to help the war effort in some way, e.g. in May 1941 the C of E Men's Bible Class arranged a dance, whist and domino drive to raise funds for the "Mothers Union Wool Fund" (to be used for knitting clothing for servicemen) and the Bible Class Comforts Fund. Many of the Co-op dances were organised by the ARP Wardens, the Civil Defence League, the Home Guard and similar organisations.

For many people the groups formed as part of the war effort also provided an important social focus. For example, the Home Guard and

AFS for men or the WVS and the knitting and sewing groups for women.

The need to reduce pressures on the transport system led to the organisation of "Holidays at Home". In June 1942 the Longridge UDC decided that activities should include a bowling handicap, 6-a-side football, dances for adults and for children, a concert and a sandpit. Large quantities of sand were brought from Lytham and a sandpit created on the recreation ground. The week appears to have been a big success. It was reported that the children were busy in the sandpit all week and over 500 were present at the children's ball in the Co-op Hall.

Preston people also rediscovered the attractions of Longridge when travelling restrictions prevented them from going further afield; e.g. Preston Mill Holiday week of August 1944 resulted in a big influx of Preston folk on buses, cycles or hiking who had adopted the "Stay close to Home" slogan.

Victory

As the allied armies swept victoriously through Europe towards Germany in 1944, it became clear that some of the wartime organisations could be disbanded and in February 1945 a social was held to mark the disbanding of the Home Guard. The Company Commander was presented with an alabaster inkstand and pen and a poem was read entitled "The Saga of the Lads of Little Lane Home Guard". This recalled "all the good times we'd had" and the foibles of various individuals. Copies were subsequently printed and sold in aid of the Red Cross Penny a Week Fund.

In May Longridge was able to join communities throughout the country in celebrating Victory in Europe with street parties, fireworks and a band on the recreation ground. On 30th May the Red Cross organised a special concert and party and invited those prisoners of war who had already been repatriated back to Longridge as guests. It was, of course, held in the Co-op Hall. After the musical items there was a good meal from reserves of food contributed by many people and poultry provided by farmers. VJ (victory over Japan) followed in August and there were further celebrations both then and as the troops returned.

Demobilisation was, however a protracted process. Bunting and "Welcome Home" signs were seen on the houses of returning service men for many months. In fact many were not able to collect their "demob suit" and return home until well into 1946. This did not, unfortunately, mean the end of the privations stemming from the war. Indeed bread had to be rationed for the first time in 1946.

However, the men were home and living conditions gradually improved. As everyone adjusted to life in post war Britain the people of Longridge could feel proud of the way in which they had coped with the difficulties, dangers and privations of the war years. From a community of just under 4000 several hundred young men and a number of young women had served their country in the armed forces, often with great distinction, far away from home. Those who remained had taken on their duties in the workplace and home and had provided hundreds of extra workers for the armaments factories. At the same time they had manned the special wartime organisations – the Home Guard, and the ARP teams, Civil Defence and AFS, Observer Corps and WVS. Hundreds more had knitted and sewed and made up parcels of comforts for servicemen and POW's. They had also collected salvage and raised funds through Church, Red Cross and other organisations on an unprecedented scale. They might feel exhausted but they could look back on the war years with pride.

ACKNOWLEDGEMENTS

Longridge and District Local History Society marked the 50th anniversary of the end of the Second World War in 1995 by tape recording the recollections of a cross section of 22 Longridge people. The recordings were made with expert guidance from Ken Howarth and Andrew Schofield of North West Sound Archives. Copies are stored both in the Sound Archives and in the Society's library. This account draws heavily on them.

It soon became apparent in preparing it that it would be impossible to name all those Longridge folk who played an important role during the war years, either in the armed forces or on the Home Front. It would be invidious to name some and not others and I therefore reluctantly concluded that I should not name anyone individually in the body of the account.

However, the contribution made to the compilation of the account by the people who tape recorded their memories is such that I feel I should thank them for their help here. They were: -

Mr Brian Bamber, who was a schoolboy during the war years and whose father, William, a grocer, was Head ARP Warden.
Mr Ted Bamber, who served in minesweepers in the North Sea amongst other duties whilst in the Royal Navy.
Mrs Elsie Cain who served in many parts of Britain in the A.T.S.
Mrs Elsie Carefoot, who taught locally and was Hon. Secretary of the Longridge branch of the Duke of Gloucester's Red Cross and St. John's Penny-a-Week Fund.
Mr. Walter Carefoot, who served in the Home Guard, and whose firm built industrial air raid shelters, carried waste material from Tootle Heights to airfields, and transported Italian POWs to farms.
Mr Chris Clegg, another member of the Home Guard, who farmed in Alston.
Mr Tom Heginbotham who was a schoolboy living in Grimsargh.
Mr Wilf Ireland, who repaired Army vehicles at Belmont Garage and was a sergeant in the Home Guard.
The late Miss Lucy Jones, who organised nurses on a countywide basis.
Mssrs John and Bernard Nolan, evacuated to Longridge from Manchester in 1939.
Mrs Edith Parkinson whose father, Mr. Jimmy Hoyle, led the Royal Observer Corps.
Ada Pinder, a weaver (Victoria Mill) and later a lathe operator (Poplar Foundry).
Harry Pinder who served as a navigator in Bomber Command.
Mr Ronald Seed who worked in the Coop initially and subsequently served in the RAF.
Mrs Elsie Singleton who was a teacher and looked after an evacuee.
Mr John Slater who served in the Army in North Africa and Italy.
Mr Wally Slater who served in the RAF in the Hebrides and in West Africa.
Mr Bill Smith, foreman at Longridge (Poplar) Foundry.
Mrs Hilda Thistleton, a weaver at Stonebridge Mill
Mrs Jean Tomlinson, a Thornley farmer's daughter, who travelled to school in Preston and later to college in Darlington.
Miss Peggy Walker, centre leader of the Longridge W.V.S.

I am are also grateful to Mr. Bernard Nichols, the late Mr John Webb, and Mr.Roger and Mrs Joan Marsden who spoke about their war experiences at the meeting which launched the project in November 1995. Mr. Nichols, whose father was Controller of the Longridge ARP during the war, served in the Army in Burma and India. John Webb too served in the Army, whilst Roger Marsden farmed locally and Joan Marsden served in the Land Army.

The other major source used in compiling this account was the "Preston Guardian" which circulated in Longridge during the war years and covered Longridge news. I am extremely grateful to Mike Keeney, the Vice Chairman of the History Society, for undertaking a thorough, detailed analysis of the back copies of this and for generously making his analysis available to me. We were able to draw on the minutes of the former Longridge Urban District Council and the logbooks of Longridge schools with the help of the County Record Office.

Mrs Jacinth Fitch and Mr A.N. Craven also provided valuable written information.

Many other people were generous in answering enquiries and in providing information and I am are grateful to them all. Particular thanks are due to the Rev. Peter Furness, President of Longridge Branch of the Royal British Legion, who made a number of the tape recordings for the Society, provided the photograph of the Pillbox and made helpful comments on the text in draft. I am also grateful to Mr Brian Bamber for the photograph of the ARP Bowls Match, to Mr Frank Salthouse for the photograph of the Joint Exercise, and to Mrs Jean Tomlinson for the photograph of Bringing in the Harvest. Mrs Tomlinson, Mr Bamber, and Mr Tom Heginbotham each made valuable comments on the text in draft.

Responsibility for the final text and for the sometimes difficult decisions about what to include and what to leave out is, however, mine.

John Earnshaw

WHITTINGHAM HOSPITAL 1873 - 1962

Harold Iddon
Introduction by Alan Dodd

Whittingham Asylum was formally opened on 1 April 1873. By the outbreak of the Second World War, over 550 staff looked after 3,533 patients in the largest mental hospital in the country. At various stages in its history, as well as medical and psychiatric facilities, it had its own church and cemetery; farms and gardens; railway and stables; telephone exchange and post office; reservoirs, gas works and power house; dairy, brewery and laundry; chaplain and blacksmiths; printers and upholsterers; orchestra and brass band; ballroom and sports teams. Its original purpose was as a county asylum "for pauper lunatics....of the ordinary classes". In the following century it underwent changes in local government and health services, was twice partly converted to a military hospital, and responded to a number of Acts of Parliament governing the admission and treatment of its patients.

In the 1940s Whittingham pioneered electro-encephalography and its application in diagnosis and therapy. In the 1960s it established the first psychiatric unit for the deaf in the United Kingdom. In moving from its original closed custodial regime to the concept of a therapeutic community, difficulties were experienced. The lack of finance, staff shortages and concerns over the treatment of patients led to a major Public Inquiry in 1971. Although the social and economic changes and the advances in patient care that contributed to its growth and decline are not unique to Whittingham, the Hospital fully merits its own chapter in the history of central Lancashire. In fact, it deserves a book to do it justice. The creation of a large institution, the equivalent of a small town, in a rural village has been a major influence on the life of the community, providing employment for generations of local people.

This article is adapted from a booklet researched and written by Harold Iddon and produced by the Hospital Management Committee, to celebrate Whittingham's centenary in 1973. Since then, the pace of change has accelerated and at the time of writing, Summer 1999, a new unit to house 54 patients is nearing completion. The final transfer of patients from existing buildings will then take place and the site will be vacated. It seems likely that the site will be developed for residential and commercial use, though the scale and nature of development and its impact on the village, is a matter of local debate and concern.

In the 19th. century tremendous strides were made in reforming the law relating to lunacy. It was not until 1845 that the Lunatic Asylum Act made the provision of asylums compulsory on the Justices of the Peace and it is from this date that mental hospitals began to appear.

The story of Whittingham Hospital began in 1866 "when all the accommodation for lunatics in Lancashire was deemed to be full". At that time, there were three asylums in the county at Prestwich, Rainhill and Lancaster, although there were other privately licensed premises.

The Reverend J. Shepherd Birley, then Chairman of Lancashire County Magistrates, and later to become first Chairman of the Committee of Visitors of Whittingham Asylum, informed the Commissioners in Lunacy of the dire need for additional accommodation, and in 1866 a Memorial proposing an additional asylum was forwarded to the Board of Finance. Records show that the Commissioners visited the locality and viewed two sites, one adjacent to Fulwood Barracks, the other at Got Field estate at Whittingham.

The Fulwood site was considered to be the better of the two, principally because of its proximity to Preston, but selection was left to the Committee of Visitors. The Committee decided on the Whittingham site which, although it was further from Preston, had easy communication with the town by the Longridge Branch railway, about one and a half miles away. It also had to access to a plentiful water supply, the land was in good condition, and it is perhaps not without significance that the asylum would be away from Fulwood Barracks and the town. In 1869 final sanction was given, the land was purchased and building commenced in the same year.

If there was any opposition to the construction of the asylum, it appears not to have been of any great significance so far as published records show. Liverpool Council voiced its opinion on the proposed size of the asylum on the grounds of economy - it was sceptical of the claimed increase in the number of lunatics in Lancashire and suggested that in any event, the increase might only be temporary, in which case a much smaller asylum would be a more reasonable proposition.

To this, the Reverend Birley and his Committee replied that "...so far back as December 1866, Memorials were presented from several Boards of Guardians to the Magistrates at the Court praying for an increase of lunacy accommodation in the County. The Memorials were referred to the Finance Committee; that Committee made diligent enquiry into the whole question of lunacy accommodation and eventually presented a most elaborate report in which it was stated that the asylums in the County were full; in addition in Haydock Lodge there were 60 pauper lunatics at the cost of 15s.0d. per week. As to the increase of lunacy, it might be a startling fact but it was one which the Court ought to know, namely that lunatics increased in Lancashire by something like 200 a year".

On behalf of the ratepayers in the area, it was suggested that the Finance Committee should act cautiously in the matter. If an asylum could be built to house 500 patients, the remainder of the money would be left in the pockets of the ratepayers until such time as additional expenditure was justified.

It was also thought that pressure should be brought to bear on appropriate authorities to prevent the number of people being brought from Dublin and left on the streets of Liverpool. If that question were to be considered, the ratepayers might be spared altogether the expense of building the asylum. At the same time, it was suggested to the Finance Committee that a great proportion of inmates in Lancashire asylums and workhouses were either Irish or foreigners, and of those admitted to Rainhill in 1868, only half were English; these "strangers" cost the County some £10,000 a year. What was not said was that a considerable proportion of the staff of Lancashire asylums were of Irish origin too!

On 29 April 1869, at the Annual General Session of the Peace for the County Palatine of Lancaster, the decision to provide a county asylum at Whittingham "for pauper lunatics" was taken under the provisions of the Lunatic Asylums Act, 1853. A committee was appointed to superintend the erection of the asylum on the site at Whittingham, which was "to be so constructed as to be capable of accommodating not fewer than 1,000 lunatic patients of the ordinary classes".

The first meeting of the Committee of Visitors of the proposed new asylum took place in the County Constabulary Office, Preston, on 7 May 1869, and the Reverend J. Shepherd Birley was appointed Chairman. The Committee's first task was to find an architect and Mr. Henry Littler, the County Architect, was appointed at "a salary after the rate of £600 per annum" and his request for assistance in the "tedious" task of preparing Bills of Quantities was granted "at the rate of £5 per week, the total sum not to exceed £50". At the same meeting, the Committee appointed its Clerk, Mr. Frederic Campbell Hulton, at a salary of £100 per annum.

Dr. Joseph Holland, Medical Superintendent at Prestwich Asylum, accepted an invitation to act as Advisor to the Committee. Dr. Holland presented to the Committee a ground plan of a proposed asylum on "the detached Block System". The plan was adopted in principle and Dr. Holland was despatched to London "to wait upon the Commissioners in Lunacy with a view to obtaining their sanction to the new asylum being built upon the system thereon described". Dr. Holland was granted the sum of £11 for preparing the plan.

The plans for the new asylum were approved in June 1869, subject to certain alterations. The Commissioners deemed it necessary to remind the architect and Dr. Holland of the importance of exercising strict economy and of avoiding "needless expense in ornament and decoration consistent with a building of pleasing and cheerful exterior, and solidarity and safety of construction". The estimated cost of the building was £105,568.16s.2d., a figure which was to be greatly exceeded. During construction, several additions and alterations to the original plan were made and the cost of materials and wages increased.

The Committee of Visitors were rebuked by the Commissioners for failing to seek their sanction to additions and changes in design.

In July 1869 contracts for the purchase of the site were approved by the Secretary of State. The site initially comprised a little over 157 acres, the cost of which was approximately £9,650 plus £200 for timber on the estate.

In September, the tender of Thomas Parsons of Whittingham was accepted for the erection of six cottages on a detached plot of land at the north east corner of the Got Field Gate estate for £1,170, and the cottages were completed and occupied by the contractor's workmen in July 1870. Later in that same year a further six cottages were erected by Cooper and Tullis of Preston, costing £1,130. All these cottages were later occupied by hospital staff.

The movement towards the asylum's construction was gathering pace. The Committee decided that bricks to be used should be manufactured on site from clay dug from the foundations and a Liverpool firm was awarded the contract, the Committee providing a shed for drying the bricks. The site from which the clay was taken was subsequently transformed from "a sand pit" to the lake in front of St. Luke's Division. In March 1870 the contract for the erection of the asylum buildings, "The Main", later known as St. Luke's, was awarded to Cooper and Tullis, their tender being the lowest at £78,550. Wells were sunk into the grounds of the estate in an unsuccessful effort to provide a water supply and eventually water was supplied by Preston Corporation at a charge of 6d. per 1,000 gallons.

In September 1871, the same contractors won the contract for the erection of a Church and Chaplain's house for £4,632 and £1,597.8s.2d. respectively, but the Chaplain's house was subsequently cancelled and was not erected until 1881 when the cost had increased to £2,000.

The asylum was rapidly becoming a reality and its approaching completion was heralded by the appointment of Dr. Holland, in December 1871, as Medical Superintendent. The appointment was to take effect from 1 May 1872, and carried a salary of £800 per annum with "house, coals, gas and washing"! Additionally, Dr. Holland was awarded a gratuity of £1,500 for his advice and services towards the design and preparation of the plans, drawings and general arrangements of the asylum.

The Committee began to consider furnishing the asylum and agreed to raise an amount not exceeding £20,000 for the purpose. At the beginning of 1872, Cooper and Tullis agreed to build lodges at the North and South entrances costing £450 and £340 respectively. A clock for the tower above the recreation hall was bought for £240 and £500 was allowed for the erection of a spire at the Church.

Midway through the year, the asylum was in part ready to take its first residents and in June 1872, permission was given for up to 50 patients to be received from Prestwich Asylum as Visitors on Leave of Absence, Prestwich being remunerated for the labour of these patients at a rate to be agreed. By September, there were 33 male and 3 female patients, the men being "regularly employed in laying out the grounds and the women in cooking and washing for them". There were two male and one female attendants.

Parts of the buildings were roofed including the Superintendent's house, the two adjacent three-storey blocks, two blocks for "excited" patients and one of the reception wards, together with the whole of the dining halls, kitchens and administrative offices including the officers' residences, and the detached laundry and workshops. The workshops and adjacent cottages cost £3,971.

By December, the patient population had increased to 115, all of whom had been transferred from Prestwich to enable that asylum "to admit 56 pauper lunatics who, for want of accommodation in the Lancashire asylums had been placed in the asylums of other counties or in private institutions at a high weekly charge of maintenance".

During the first three months of 1873, the work necessary to enable the asylum to be opened officially was completed. Mr. Thomas Dilworth became Treasurer, Clerk and Steward, at an annual salary of £200 with board and lodging for himself, wife and child, and a Medical Officer was appointed at a salary of £100 with board and lodging provided. An Engineer, Mr. James Kirkham, was appointed at a weekly wage of £1.14s.0d. with house, coal and gas, and Mr. Henry Barleycorn became Head Attendant after having spent 22 years as attendant at Prestwich.

The Committee decided that the Whittingham Asylum would be formally opened on 1 April 1873. The weekly sums to be charged for lodging, maintenance, medicine, clothing and care of each pauper lunatic confined in the Asylum were 9s.11d. per head for patients from Townships and Unions within the County, and 14s.0d. per head for those who originated from other Counties.

The formal opening of the Asylum appears to have passed without any attendant ceremony, perhaps because the contractors were well behind schedule for the completion of the building.

An organ was purchased and installed in the Church at a cost of £250 and arrangements were made "to warm the Church with hot water heated by gas". In October, Ellen Tomkinson and Ann Hurst, attendants at Prestwich Asylum, were appointed Chief Female Officer and Housekeeper respectively, each receiving an annual salary of £45.

By the end of the year, expenditure on building and furnishing the Asylum had mounted to £137,976, and application had been made for a further £35,000 in order to complete the building. The patient population had increased to 304 - 154 males and 150 females.

The development of the Asylum was, of course, a continuing process and during the years that followed provision was made for the erection of cottages for gardening staff, farm buildings and the installation of steam boilers. A room in a ward was set aside for the celebration of Divine Service for Roman Catholic patients and the visiting priest was paid 15s.0d. a week for travelling expenses. Rent of cottages occupied by attendant staff was fixed at 2s.6d. per week with water and free from rates and taxes but with no allowances for gas or coal. Dr. Squire, the Senior Assistant Medical Officer, successfully applied to the Committee "that he be allowed to marry and that accommodation be provided for himself and wife within the asylum". He was charged an annual sum of £25 board and lodging.

By the end of 1874, the available accommodation for patients had increased to 600 beds of which 571 were occupied and expenditure had amounted to £168,668. It was expected the asylum would be completed during 1875 and accommodate 1,100 patients. The Committee's report for the year noted that "as the patients for the most part had been drafted from other asylums and whose malady was rather of a confirmed than of a hopeful class, a high percentage of cures could not be reasonably expected".

The asylum was completed in June 1875, and ready to receive its full complement of patients. The Church was licensed by the Bishop of Manchester for the performance of Divine Service, and the first Rules and Regulations for Attendants were printed. The Rules are far too lengthy to be reprinted here but they make interesting reading. For example, all attendants were to commence their duties at 6.00 a.m. and to retire to bed at 10.00 p.m. They were allowed to go out one day in every three weeks after 9.00 a.m. and on one Sunday in each month after the same hour. Any attendant who had the misfortune to "lose" a patient was expected to pay the expenses incurred in returning him.

The Main Building c.1877

Considering the dreadful treatment of the mentally disordered in the centuries preceding the erection of Whittingham Asylum, the rules and regulations, which were modelled on those in force at Prestwich Asylum, were remarkable for the standards they set in regard to the care and treatment of the patients.

At the beginning of 1876, the number of patients was 891 and the cost of the asylum had increased to £191,260. Attendant staff increased during the year to 55 males, recruited at wages ranging from £55 to £23 per year, and there were 50 female attendants whose wages were somewhat lower, ranging from £30 to £20 a year. Medical staff comprised the Superintendent and two assistants. It was clear then that the asylum as it stood would not be large enough to cope with the expected growth in the patient population, and in 1877 the Committee sought surrounding land on which to build an Annexe capable of holding 600 patients, subsequently acquiring Dale Brow Farm on a 14 years' lease at an annual rent of £80.

In the following year, with the patients now exceeding 1,100, some 68 acres were purchased at a cost of £105 an acre, and the tender of Cooper and Tullis amounting to £49,000 was accepted for the construction of a building to accommodate 700 patients. This building later became known as St. John's. The Committee now produced and adopted its "Rules for the Government of the Asylum".

In August 1878, Dr. Holland, the Medical Superintendent, who had been associated with the Asylum since its beginning, retired and was succeeded by Dr. John A. Wallis from the Hull Borough Asylum. Dr. Holland was born in 1813 and studied at King's College and St. George's Hospitals, London, before practising in Chorlton, near Manchester. He became Research Medical Officer at the Surrey Lunatic Asylum and in 1855 was appointed Medical Superintendent at Prestwich Lunatic Asylum.

Much of the success which the Asylum enjoyed was due to Dr. Holland, and Burdett in his "Hospitals and Asylums of the World" (Volume 2) wrote of Whittingham : "This is beyond doubt one of the finest specimens of asylum architecture in England and its leading features show at once that it was designed by a Medical Superintendent". Burdett listed several criticisms but, nevertheless, concluded his narrative by saying that, "In spite of these drawbacks no one should think of designing an asylum without first studying Whittingham".

By now, the final cost of "The Main" - St. Luke's - had risen to £179,973 with furnishings accounting for a further £21,000 although of course these figures included certain ancillary buildings and stables in which the medical officers accommodated their horses.

In 1879, the weekly in-county maintenance rate was reduced to 9s.4d. per head, the patient population was 1,244 and work had begun on new sewerage works. Two new appointments had been made, Mr. W. Haldane as Farm Bailiff and Mr. W. H. Stevenson as Foreman of Works. Mr. Rowbotham, at that time Superintendent of Preston Corporation Parks' Staff, had been appointed to lay out the Asylum grounds for which he was to be paid £25 a year for upwards of 8 years.

1880 saw a further reduction of 7d. in the weekly maintenance rate for in-county patients. Satisfactory progress was being made towards the completion of the new Annexe, and it already accommodated 115 patients. It is clear from the records that the members of the Committee were extremely diligent in their approach to the administration and development of Whittingham. Plans for the enlargement of the farm buildings were approved, the Chaplain's House was begun, and the Committee contributed a sum of £15,500 towards the construction and maintenance of waterworks at Beacon Fell in the Township of Goosnargh and Newsham, on condition that the Asylum received 90,000 gallons a day free of charge. This arrangement led subsequently to the Fulwood and Whittingham Water Act of 1882.

The Chaplain's House was completed in 1882 and occupied by the Rev. W. T. Palmour and his family. By the end of the year the Annexe had also been finished and housed 509 patients, bringing the total population of the Asylum to 1,648. A Head Nurse and a Principal Nurse had been appointed for the Annexe together with a Chief Night Attendant and a Superintendent of Laundry/Deputy Principal Nurse. The gas works were extended at a cost of £2,000, the amount of gas produced and consumed during the year being 5 million cubic feet.

1883 saw the resignation as Chairman of the Rev. J. Shepherd Birley on grounds of failing health and, regrettably, he died later in the year. His place as Chairman was taken by Mr. Charles Roger Jacson who was to resign in the following year after a difference of opinion over an increase in the annual salary of the Chaplain. The salaries of the principal officers of the Asylum were reviewed during this year. The Medical Superintendent was granted an increase of £400 per annum with "house, coals, gas, water, washing, and vegetables grown in the hospital grounds". The Chaplain's rise was £100 per annum with perquisites similar to the Medical Superintendent, and the Clerk, Steward and Treasurer also having an extra £100 a year with the same "perks". The Senior Assistant Medical Officer's salary was raised by £50 to £200 a year. A "duly registered Pharmaceutical Chemist" was appointed as Dispenser.

The Postmaster General agreed to the establishment of a "Provincial Post Office" in the Asylum, subsequently sited in one of the cottages, and plans were approved for the erection of an Infectious Diseases Hospital for 16 patients at an estimated cost of £3,500. This building, completed in 1886, was later to be called the Sanatorium, and, later still, Fryars' Villa, renamed after Alderman James Fryars, Chairman of the Committee from 1933 to 1952, and used as staff accommodation.

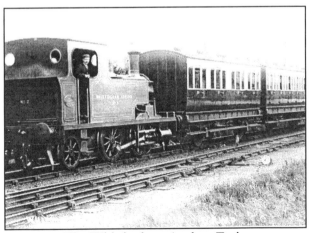

The Whittingham Asylum Train

The Fulwood Water Board had successfully sought permission to take water from the pipes supplying the Asylum in order to provide water for the village of Goosnargh from the Asylum's reservoirs, which then had a capacity of 52 million gallons.

In September, Whittingham Hall Estate, comprising the farm, Stags Head Inn and blacksmith's shop, was offered for sale, but two bids made by the Committee - of £11,500 and £12,000 - were rejected. The estate was again up for sale in 1889, and this time the Committee's offer of £9,500 for part of the land was accepted. By the end of 1883 the patient population had increased to 1,767, and the Committee had decided to instal "not more than 12" gas lamp-posts in the grounds.

In 1884, "telephonic" communication with Preston was established at an annual cost of £20 by means of a private exchange run by a Mr. Sharples of Preston. The Chaplain's salary was increased to £400 a year, a move which so incensed the Chairman, Mr. C. R. Jacson, that he resigned from the Committee and was succeeded as Chairman by the Reverend Charles T. Royds. 20,000 bricks were sold to the Vicar of Goosnargh for the enlargement of the Vicarage.

The Committee began seriously to consider a railway line or horse - drawn tramway from the Asylum to Grimsargh for the conveyance of goods and passenger traffic, relatives and friends of patients, and the public generally. 1886 saw the purchase of land - approximately 11½ acres - for the construction of a private railway to Grimsargh for which the owners were to be compensated to a total not exceeding £3,000. The land eventually cost £2,310, and £10,000 was granted for construction with, later, a further £5,000 for the purchase of rolling stock - an engine and two goods vans. Construction of the railway began in 1887, and in the following year an engine was bought for £780 from Barclays of Kilmarnock.

Accommodation was now to be provided in the Asylum for non-pauper lunatics (private patients), for which the weekly maintenance rate was fixed at not less than 14s.0d. weekly. In 1885 the rate for in-county patients was restored to 9s.4d. a week, influenced perhaps by the fact that genuine butter was to be provided to the exclusion of butterine.

The patient population was 1,688, and a lease of Haighton House Farm and Haighton Hall containing some 104 acres was taken for 21 years at £200 a year.

The Local Government Act, 1888, established County and County Borough Councils and took away from the justices the administration of asylums. Thus, Whittingham Asylum became vested in the Lancashire County Council, subject to certain rights of representation on the Committee of Management of representatives of those local authorities who had contributed to the cost of constructing the Asylum. In 1889 a Sub-Committee was appointed for the management of Whittingham Asylum, of which Mr. C. R. Jacson was appointed Chairman and Mr. W. J. Fitzherbert-Brockholes, Vice-Chairman. The patient population totalled 1,789 of which the Main Building housed 1,144 and the Annexe 645.

1890, the year of the Lunacy Act, one of the great pieces of social legislation, saw the installation of a direct telephone line to Garstang Police Station, the enlargement of the gas works and the appointment of an assistant in Pathology. Mr. C. Hulton, Clerk to the Committee since 1869, resigned and was succeeded by Mr. John P. Muspratt.

Female Attendants in the Day Room, c.1900

The Lancashire County (Lunatic and Other Powers) Act 1891, constituted an Asylums Board for the County Palatine of Lancaster and vested existing County Lunatic Asylums in the Board.

In 1892, Mr. Jacson resigned as Chairman on grounds of ill-health and was succeeded by County Alderman Fitzherbert-Brockholes. The Committee, conscious of the fact that the available accommodation was insufficient to cope with the demand - the patients now totalled 1,857 - began to consider plans for the provision of a further 200 beds for reception, acute wards and additional staff accommodation, estimated to cost about £30,000. For reasons which are not clear the scheme was postponed. The use of electricity for lighting the grounds was approved and £5,000 was allocated for the purpose. External iron staircases (fire escapes) were erected to dormitories at a cost of £1,850. There was a shortage of patient labour for the farms and successful approaches were made to the three other county asylums for the transfer of some 120 male patients to assist in the farm work.

The next twenty years produced many developments in the administration and staffing at Whittingham. With the patient population numbering 1,936, the medical staff comprised the Superintendent, four assistant medical officers and a pathologist. In 1893 Dr. Wallis, who had been Medical Superintendent since 1878, resigned on appointment as a Commissioner in Lunacy and was succeeded by Dr. F. Perceval from Prestwich Asylum.

The question of additional accommodation was reconsidered and this time approved, and in 1895 the building of a new hospital - later known as Cameron House, after Alderman Cameron Doodson, Chairman of the Hospital Management Committee - was commenced at an estimated cost of £40,490 including furnishings, the contractors being Thomas Croft of Preston.

The asylum cemetery was consecrated by the Bishop of Manchester, and subsequently the Hospital Chaplain was awarded 2s.6d. for each burial service performed.

It is interesting to note that some difficulty had arisen in 1870 between the Visiting Magistrates and the Vicar and Churchwardens of Goosnargh. The Church authorities were anxious to limit burials in

Goosnargh Cemetery to those members of families already buried there. A letter from the Burial Acts Office in London to the Committee stated that "the proposed enlargement of the (Goosnargh) Churchyard would be cancelled unless the parishioners were assured that deceased inmates of the Lunatic Asylum not belonging to the Parish were buried elsewhere".

The Clerk to the Committee replied that inmates had the right to be buried in the Churchyard since they were residing in the area, and that if they were not allowed to be buried there an additional Churchyard would have to be provided. He also stated: "The conduct of the Vicar and Churchwardens on this matter can only be contemplated by the Committee of Visitors as exhibiting a feeling of hostility towards the unfortunate inmates of the asylum and as an attempt to evade their own respective duties and responsibilities which it is sincerely hoped that it may not be necessary to compel them legally to fulfil. The Committee of Visitors have no intention whatever to provide a separate burial ground for the insane".

Female attendents sewing c.1900

1899 saw the erection of iron gates at North Lodge, extensions and alterations to the laundry including the installation of electric lighting, and the addition to the medical staff of two assistant medical officers. At the turn of the century Cameron House was occupied by patients, bringing the total at Whittingham to 2,103. Free passes were introduced on the asylum railway. The Senior Assistant Medical Officer, Dr. Alexander Simpson, left to become Medical Superintendent at the new Asylum in Winwick.

In 1901 the maintenance rate was increased from 8s.9d. to 9s.4d. and attendants and servants were granted an allowance of 10s.0d. per week in lieu of rations whilst they were away on annual leave. The attendants began to agitate for a shorter working week, the hours at the time being 98¼ (including meal times) with one day off in every three weeks and one Sunday off in every four. Annual leave amounted to 10 days in the case of attendants, 12 days for Second Charges and 14 days for Charge Attendants.

Dr. Perceval resigned as Medical Superintendent to take a similar appointment at Prestwich and was succeeded on 1 January 1902 by Dr. J. F. Gemmel.

Male Attendants c.1905

For some years there had been a brewery in the Asylum grounds. To what extent it was regarded as a therapeutic necessity to the hospital is not clear but the daily diet of patients and staff included one glass of ale. Whether or not the facility was abused is a matter of conjecture, but records show that from time to time it was necessary to discipline - and sometimes dismiss - members of staff for drunkenness on duty. For whatever reason, the Committee were moved to discontinue its existence from September 1902, and to grant monetary allowances to staff "in lieu of beer and milk".

In 1903 the designation of the post of Clerk, Steward and Treasurer was changed to Clerk and Steward, and the Preston Branch of the Lancaster Banking Company was appointed to act as Treasurers to the Asylum.

The patient population - 2,072 - had remained virtually static since 1899 and showed little variation during succeeding years.

In 1906 the Committee built a new railway station costing £600 and purchased new carriages for £220.

Part of the buildings which had formerly housed the now disused brewery was occupied by upholsterers and printers, and once again the Committee began to consider the possibility of extending the accommodation to house a further 700 patients. Architects within the County were invited to submit plans, designs and estimates for which prizes of £100, £50 and £25 were offered. Messrs. Sykes and Evans of Manchester were awarded first prize for the design of a new annexe for chronic patients, later named St. Margaret's.

The report of the Commissioners in Lunacy for 1909 commented that "In an Institution of this character, where everything continues to be maintained in such a high state of efficiency, there is little for us to say beyond an expression of our great satisfaction with all that we have seen during our visit".

In 1910 the Committee purchased Haighton House Farm comprising 104 acres for £5,600 which brought the area of land owned by the Hospital to 621 acres.

The administration and staffing of Whittingham had been smoothly effective from the beginning, but in 1911 the Committee were somewhat dismayed to receive a report from the Medical Superintendent "that a circular had been issued to the male attendants and servants of the asylum inviting them to join an Asylum Officers' Union". It appeared that a meeting "had been held at the Annexe in connection with the matter and that such meeting was held without proper sanction or authority".

The Fire Brigade outside the Fire Station in the grounds, c.1910

That the Committee was disturbed by the event is shown by the terms of the resolution it adopted. It was of the opinion that the attendants and servants had reasonable opportunities to ventilate and obtain redress of any grievances; that some of the principles set out in the circular were calculated to interfere with the necessary and proper discipline of the asylum and that those responsible for calling the meeting were deserving of censure. The Committee instructed the Medical Superintendent to deal with any attendant or servant of the asylum actively identifying himself with the principles in the circular and to report to the Committee.

What, if any, action was taken by the Medical Superintendent is not recorded, but the General Secretary of the National Asylum Workers Union clearly regarded it as "antagonistic". Subsequently he wrote to

the Committee asking whether there was any objection to the staff
becoming members of the Union, and whether membership would prove
prejudicial to their prospects in the Institution. The Committee avoided
a decision by asking the Medical Superintendent to suggest "how best
the question might be brought to the attention of the Lancashire
Asylums Board" with a view to the Board raising the matter with the
Lunacy Commissioners and the Home Secretary.

The Orchestra, c.1914

It was not until April 1914 that the Board of Control indicated that as
the matter was one of considerable importance, and likely to be the
subject of a petition to Parliament, the Home Secretary would need
further information. The Board was anxious to know whether, apart
from any rule or understanding on the use of "threats or intimidation",
employees were informed either by the Visiting Committee or the
Medical Superintendent that they would not be allowed to join a trade
union. At this point the Committee decided it would be prudent "as the
Medical Superintendent has control over employees" to refer the letter
to him for reply.

Meanwhile further progress was being made with the development of
additional accommodation. Building of the West Annexe had begun in
1912 when the patient population was 2,094 and the ratio of staff to
patients was 1:8.6. In 1913 new machinery for the laundry was bought

at a cost of £2,000, new kitchen plant cost £1,206, additions to the engine rooms and boiler house accounted for a further £1,580 and electrical installations cost £9,442. £7,000 was spent on clothing and bedding and £14,000 was allocated for furniture for the new Annexe. The purchase of a plot of land dividing the Asylum estate from the Preston to Longridge highway cost £520.

Corridor Ward, St. Luke's, with decorations c.1915

1913 also saw the departure of the Senior Assistant Medical Officer to Whalley Asylum where he became Medical Superintendent.

In the following year the Recreation Hall was enlarged, and virtually rebuilt, at a cost of £6,300. Clearly there was a difference of opinion for the committee resolved that they would not agree with any suggestion of the Commissioners which would entail abolition of the Clock Tower. The West Annexe was opened by the Chairman, Alderman J. Miles, in October 1914, but no formal invitations for the occasion were issued.

By the end of 1915, the patient population had increased to 2,820 primarily due to the transfer of 547 patients from Winwick Asylum to the West Annexe, Winwick having been converted to a military hospital. Over 100 of the staff, including four assistant medical officers, joined the Forces and the resident medical staff was reduced to the Superintendent, two permanent and four locum medical officers.

At the end of the war, the West Annexe was vacated and converted into a military hospital for the treatment of sick and wounded soldiers, most of the women patients originating from Winwick having since been transferred to other institutions. So by the end of 1918 the number of patients had reduced to 1,976.

Whittingham Hospital was now virtually at its greatest extent, the only major works of construction being the future extensions to the West Annexe and the addition of the Nurse Training School. The Committee, nevertheless, continued to ensure that the Asylum was run on the most beneficial lines, and that there was no lack of humanity and compassion in the treatment of those whose illness necessitated admission.

In the immediate post-war years, one of the most exciting developments in the treatment of mental illness followed the introduction, in 1917 by Dr. Jauregg of Vienna, of treatment of general paralysis of the insane (neuro-syphilis) by induced malaria fever. It was at Whittingham in 1922 that the treatment was first tried in England and it revolutionised the outlook for remission of mental illness.

By 1923 the Committee records were referring to Whittingham Mental Hospital, and the number of patients had increased to 2,789 with a nursing staff of 350. The staff working hours were increased from 48 to 54 and annual leave to three weeks. Additional cottages were built for staff and new roads were constructed in the grounds. In the following year the Commissioners of the Board of Control commented "with some surprise" that there was "no one official in the position of Matron at this hospital" and suggested that one "fully trained in general hospital as well as mental nursing would prove a most valuable step".

The Commissioners added that in view of the proximity of the Queen Victoria Royal Infirmary at Preston, it might be found practicable to establish in the out-patient department there a section for mental and neurological disorders, and that for the treatment of such patients in the early stages of such illnesses the skilled services of medical staff at Whittingham might be available.

Tables laid out for patients c.1915

The Commissioners noted in 1929 that a number of wards were administered on the "open door" principle. The implementation of the Local Government Act of that year abolished Boards of Guardians and transferred administration of the Poor Law to counties and county boroughs.

A canteen for the convenience of patients' visitors was started, and artisan and labouring staffs applied for holidays with pay, an application which the Committee viewed with favour and passed to the Lancashire Asylums Board.

In 1930 Parliament passed the Mental Treatment Act. The Board of Control was re-constituted and for the first time admission of voluntary patients to mental hospitals was permitted. The Act provided for the "temporary" detention of patients on medical recommendation for a period not exceeding one year, thus avoiding the stigma of certification. It introduced new terminology: "Asylum" was replaced by "Mental Hospital" - a measure anticipated at Whittingham by several years - and "lunatic" was replaced by "person of unsound mind".

Prior to the 1930 Act, all patients were admitted to asylums on a certificate prepared on the order of a Justice of the Peace. For the most part these patients came from hospitals administered by the Guardians of the Poor of Parishes or Unions of Parishes. The Relieving Officer, the counterpart of the later Mental Welfare or Social Services Officer, was responsible for arranging a medical certificate and for a Justice of the Peace to receive the certificate and sign the order as required by the Lunacy Act, 1890, for the patient's reception into a mental hospital.

In 1932 the patient population exceeded 3,000 for the first time. Staff numbered 433 and the Commissioners of the Board of Control paid tribute to "the high standards prevailing in every department of this great Institution".

A psychiatric out-patient clinic started at Preston Royal Infirmary and an Occupational Therapy department began to operate in the Main division. The first voluntary and temporary patients were admitted in 1933.

The 1930 Act was intended to, and did, promote much to enable out-patient clinics to discover and give early treatment to cases of mental illness. It emphasised the desirability of in-patient treatment being succeeded by adequate community care after discharge. In turn, this meant the speedier development of rehabilitation facilities within the hospital.

Since its beginning, Whittingham had had its own orchestra and, later, its own brass band. Both attained an extremely high standard and their membership included several patients from the hospital. Sunday afternoon concerts and pantomimes became a popular feature of local life and were well attended by the community.

During his period as Medical Superintendent (1920 - 1931), Dr. R. M. Clark had done much to foster this kind of "social" activity which he believed to be of great therapeutic value.

Kitchen in 1920s.
Staff member using porridge funnel

His successor, Dr. A. R. Grant (1931-1956), a sports enthusiast, continued and extended these activities. He encouraged the recruitment of staff with sporting ability, on the premise that the more involved staff became in the day-to-day life of the hospital, the more patients would benefit. Whittingham Hospital, therefore, in the 1930s, developed a sporting tradition of which it is still justifiably proud. It had rugby union, football and cricket teams and a ladies hockey team, each of which played fixtures at a high competitive level and enjoyed considerable success.

The "open door" principle was maintained and extended and several hundred patients had access not only to the spacious and well-manicured grounds of the hospital but also to the village community.

Psychiatric out-patient clinics commenced at Blackburn and new arrangements were made for consultants in other specialities, e.g. surgery, radiology, orthopaedics, ophthalmology to attend the hospital. At the outbreak of the Second World War the patient population numbered 3,533 and Whittingham was said by the Commissioners to be the "largest Mental Hospital in the country".

Dairy Interior, c.1930

Its medical staff comprised a Superintendent and deputy, two senior assistants and five assistant medical officers, and the nursing staff totalled 548. The Nurses' Home opened in 1939 and almost all the wards had "wireless" installed.

In the months preceding war, the Civil Defence Bill had outlined arrangements for Emergency Medical Services in order to meet any demand by air-raid casualties. As a result wards 31 to 36 were vacated and this part became known as "Whittingham Emergency Hospital". It contained 900 beds and many casualties, both military and civilian as well as prisoners of war, were treated there, the first major casualties being from Dunkirk. Administrative charge of the hospital was in the hands of the Medical Superintendent, Dr. Grant, who in turn was responsible to the Ministry of Health Emergency Medical Services office in Manchester. A Major of the Royal Army Medical Corps was responsible for military discipline and had his own complement of military personnel.

Butcher's Shop, Christmas 1938.
Christmas Dinner was 8 sheep, 6 pigs, 4 bullocks and 38 turkeys

Tribute must be paid to the Emergency Services Medical staff under the direction of Mr. A. Sutcliffe Kerr, Surgeon, whose devotion to the patients caused him to be known as "the man who never slept"; to the staff of the Civil Nursing Reserve; to the staff of the mental hospital who gave unstintingly of their services; and to many local voluntary organisations which provided the extra comforts so welcome to patients and staff.

The Emergency Hospital was vacated by the military during 1946 and the accommodation resumed its proper function, the population being 3,183. This year saw the passing of the National Health Service Act, as a result of which mental hospitals became vested in the Minister of Health, and psychiatry found a place as a speciality.

The Act provided for the integration of the mental and personal health services, the intention being to promote a comprehensive service designed to secure an improvement in the physical and mental health of the community.

The country was divided into regions, the purpose of which was to administer the hospital, consultant and specialist services free of charge to the consumer except where otherwise provided. Regional Hospital Boards were established responsible to the Minister for the administration of the hospitals within their areas, with the exception of the Teaching Hospitals which were the responsibility of Boards of Governors. The Regional Hospital Boards, in turn, set up Hospital Management Committees responsible for the day-to-day administration of the hospitals within their groups.

In 1946 the Committee decided to provide funds to establish a department of electro-encephalography. The Medical Superintendent approached Dr. C. S. Parker with a view to obtaining an E. E. G. machine. Electro-encephalograhy was a new development and there were no commercial models available in this country. Mr. Charles Breakell, then part-time Dental Surgeon at Whittingham and a radio "ham", was an enthusiast for electronic "gadgetry", having spent a great deal of his war service on radar. He and Dr. Parker discussed the possibility of constructing an E. E. G. machine from war surplus electronic apparatus, then being disposed of in large quantities at something like £2.10s.0d. a hundredweight.

Eventually, having persuaded the Ministry to grant the necessary permit to purchase the "scrap", Dr. Parker and Mr. Breakell hired a farmer's truck and scoured the Liverpool dock area and other depots from which Mr. Breakell selected the parts needed.

Before beginning to assemble their machine, they both went on a course to Burden Neurological Intitute, Bristol, under Dr. Grey Walter, the leading authority on electro-encephalography, who provided them with a great deal of moral support and encouragement as well as excellent tuition.

An E. E. G. machine was eventually constructed and after many set - backs it produced a "rhythm". Great difficulty was experienced for a time due to feedback between the patient and the machine. However, when they were placed on opposite sides of the room, the result was the first E. E. G. tracing. Later, a service was established at Whittingham for the north-west of England.

Mr. Frank Christopherson, who had been working on police radio, joined the team and a portable transmitter was developed, allowing the patient to move around, and also incorporating an electro - cardiograph.

In 1949, a paper was submitted to "the Lancet", describing the "Transmission of Brain Waves", which excited so much attention from the national press and the B.B.C. that hordes of reporters descended on the hospital.

The article also aroused the interest of the recently formed American Department of Space Medicine, who hoped to apply the principles to monitor the brain and heart rhythms of astronauts, and subsequently this method became a regular practice in space flights.

The work of Dr. Parker and his team in medical electronics later led to developments in behaviour therapy for the treatment of phobic and other neurotic conditions.

On 5 July 1948, the date of implementation of the National Health Service Act, the Lancashire Mental Hospitals Board was dissolved, Whittingham Hospital Management Committee was appointed, and Ribchester Hospital, originally constructed in 1823 as a Workhouse, became part of the Whittingham Group.

At the inaugural meeting of the Management Committee in June 1948, Mr. W. A. Higgs, then Clerk and Steward, was appointed Secretary/ Finance Officer/Supplies Officer. In 1949 this appointment was varied. Mr. Higgs became Secretary to the Management Committee and Supplies Officer, and Mr. F. Riding, formerly Deputy Clerk and Steward, became Treasurer.

The patient population, with Ribchester, was now 3,235 and the maintenance rate £3.1s.3d. per week.

For the Coronation in 1953, the Management Committee allocated £440 for the provision of extra amenities for patients to mark the event. Later in the year several wards had television sets installed, a project completed in 1956. The existing accommodation was extended and improved, 14 staff houses were built at a cost of £33,771, including roads and sewers. £44,850 was allowed for the renewal of hot water supply mains at St. Luke's and St. John's Divisions and £11,600 for the modernisation of wards 8 and 16. Permission was given for the conversion of the Medical Superintendent's house into a Patients' Social Centre, later known as 'The Lawns', at an estimated cost of £4,250. A new house for the Medical Superintendent was erected the following year for £5,231.

Along with other mental hospitals, Whittingham was experiencing a serious shortage of nursing staff. Advertisements placed abroad had brought recruits from Italy, France, Denmark and Malta, but more were needed. In 1956 a deputation on behalf of 11 hospitals in the Manchester and Liverpool Regions, led by the Chairman of the Whittingham H.M.C., was received by the Minister of Health in London.

On a visit to Whittingham in February, the Minister, the Rt. Hon. Robin Turton, spent over three hours touring the hospital, talked to staff and management about their problems, and called the staff social club "as nice a club as I have seen anywhere on my visits". He felt that the answer to staff shortages lay in improving amenities, and already the Regional Hospital Board had considered plans which included improved heating, painting and modernisation.

For the first time in many years, it had not been possible to hold the annual Pantomime in the ballroom the previous Christmas due to staff shortages. Despite these difficulties, the staff managed impromptu functions and events including dances, whist drives, concerts, film shows, outings and other social activities.

It was to their credit that the considerably overworked staff did their best to improve the comfort and entertainment of patients.

Ballroom showing stage and decorated pillars

Joe Davis, the world professional snooker champion, visited the hospital and demonstrated his skills to patients and staff on a snooker table specially erected in the ballroom.

Later in the year £30,000 was made available for alterations to the kitchens and staff cafeteria, and for the first stage of the reconstruction of the power house, the whole scheme costing over £250,000.

One of the features of Whittingham Hospital since its beginning, had been the amount of farming activity on the estate. In 1955, 564 acres were farmed but the Regional Board recommended the disposal of 260 acres. A deputation from the Management Committee visited the Ministry of Health in London to oppose the recommendation.

The Committee, like their predecessors, were justifiably proud of the part played by the farms in the hospital's development, because of the amount of foodstuffs produced for hospital use and also because of the facilities the farms provided for patients to be usefully and therapeutically occupied. During his 30 years as Farm Manager, Mr. James Allsup had built up a famous pedigree herd of "Large White" pigs, and a feature of local life was the annual pig sale attended by buyers from far and wide. The Regional Board had also recommended that the herd should be sold.

The result of the deputation was a compromise. It was agreed that the herd should be halved to 250, and the acreage owned by the hospital reduced. New Chingle Hall Farm (119 acres), Haighton Green Lane land (23 acres) and Cumeragh Lane land (21 acres) were sold.

In 1956 Dr. Grant retired as Medical Superintendent, a post he had held since 1931, his total service at the hospital being 42 years.

The Management Committee had made further representations to the Regional Board that Whittingham was inadequately staffed with medical officers as compared with other mental hospitals, and requested an increase in the medical establishment. Patient numbers, including Ribchester, were over 3,000. Although more money was being spent on upgrading of wards and improvements in ancillary services, the Committee questioned the Board's priorities in allocating finance.

1957 saw the inaugural meeting of the Hospital Nurse Training, later Nurse Education, Committee. Accommodation for nurse training comprised a lecture room in Cameron House and a demonstration room at ward 46, really quite insufficient for the purpose. The Management Committee approved plans for the upgrading and centralisation of the School at Cameron House at a cost of £4,850.

The year also saw the passing of the Whittingham Hospital Railway, a matter of considerable regret to the Management Committee and the hospital staff. It was a private line, constructed in 1887 by Lancashire County Council to connect the hospital with the nearest railway at Grimsargh, to transport coal and other goods. Passenger trains ran primarily for the benefit of hospital staff and patients' visitors, the service being free of charge. At one time, the railway had carried hundreds of visitors each week, but with the inauguration of a direct bus service to Whittingham village few visitors used the service.

The railway track was some 2 miles in length, had no signals, gradient posts or mile posts and the passenger vehicles had no brakes. It ran from a small station with a single platform in the hospital grounds. The passenger service ran about 12 times a day at a speed of 12 - 13 miles an hour, burning 10 shovelfuls of coal each journey. It was not unknown for the driver to halt the train, cross the line and feed his poultry on land adjacent to the track. During the 68 years of its life, six locomotives were used, the last bought from Bolton Gas Works in 1947.

The passing of the railway marked the end of an era in which costs had been secondary to comfort and convenience, and gave way to an age in which public transport authorities failed to match the needs of staff and visitors to the hospital. The last journey on the railway was on 30 June 1957, and from that time the Committee had to arrange for a private bus service from Whittingham to Grimsargh for staff.

Alderman Cameron W. Doodson resigned as Chairman of the Management Committee in 1957 and was succeeded by Alderman James Vickers of Bolton, and Dr. W. A. M. Robinson was appointed Medical Superintendent.

The hospital estate was again reduced, with Pigot House Farm (75 acres) and Lodge Fields (20 acres), adjacent to Chingle Hall Farm, being vacated on the expiration of the Committee's lease.

1958 saw the official renaming of the various hospital divisions. "The Main" became St. Luke's, "West Annexe" became St. Margaret's and "The Annexe" became St. John's.

The Management Committee were increasingly conscious of the hospital's place in the community. In 1959 it welcomed the formation of the Whittingham League of Friends, arising out of approaches made by the Standing Conference of Women's Organisations in Preston, whose members, together with those of other organisations, had been engaged in selective visiting of patients for some time.

One-day shops were arranged with the co-operation of two of the leading stores in Preston. The hospital ballroom was placed at their disposal and they displayed clothing and toiletries which the patients could buy.

The hospital adopted as its crest the Red Rose of Lancashire with the motto "Fide et Fortitudine". The crest was incorporated in the Hospital Badge and Certificate awarded at the Annual Nurses' Prize- Giving Day to student and pupil nurses who successfully completed their training.

Male nursing staff began to wear dark grey suits instead of the uniform which had been traditional for many years. Gaberdine raincoats and hats were provided for female staff.

The Committee began to intensify development of occupational therapy and rehabilitation services. A social worker and Education Officer (later Social Therapist) were appointed, and consideration was given to the setting up of a Rehabilitation Group comprising representatives of medical, nursing and therapy staffs.

Wards 17 and 18 were upgraded in 1959 at a cost of £70,000, a new staff restaurant was opened in St. Luke's, and the Staff Social Club was enlarged for £4,000, of which the club itself contributed £1,750.

In 1961 the Management Committee submitted to the Regional Board its proposals for development during the next 10 years, including the major remodelling of four wards, upgrading of heating and laundry services and the adaptation of accommodation to allow for improved occupational and industrial rehabilitation services.

Developments over the next few years were to be governed by the "Hospital Plan for England and Wales", presented to Parliament by the Minister of Health in 1962. Its implications for the region and the future of psychiatric provision anticipated the major health service reorganisation of 1974 and heralded a new chapter in the story of Whittingham Hospital.

LIBRARIES IN THE LONGRIDGE AREA: 1684-1964

Mike Pattinson

To many of the newer residents of Longridge and district, the County Branch Library in Berry Lane, opened in 1964, represents the public library service in the town. It does not follow, however, that before this date no provision was made for public access to books, newspapers and periodicals. Such provision has existed in various forms in Britain since the Middle Ages, though the modern public library system only dates from 1850.

The 19th. century inherited three types of libraries from earlier periods: the endowed libraries, mainly religious and attached to churches; libraries in cathedrals and learned societies; subscription libraries, private and commercial.[1] By 1850 the endowed libraries were in decline. A notable local exception was the Shepherd Library in Preston, which had its own building and librarian, and after the Municipal Reform Act of 1835 was open not only in the daytime from 10.00 a.m. to 4.00 p.m., but also, unusually for early libraries, from 6.00 p.m. to 9.45 p.m. in the evenings. It was accessible to anyone on application to one of the trustees, and, from 1839, on the payment of 3s. for a copy of the printed catalogue. 10,000 volumes survive in the Harris Library.[2]

A special feature of the early 19th. century was the increasing library provision for working people. Despite Lancashire's tradition of grammar schools, few working-class children received any education, and levels of literacy were to remain low until the Education Act of 1870 made elementary education compulsory. Nevertheless, libraries multiplied and played an essential part in a variety of philanthropic and mutual improvement societies. These institutions included co-operative societies, trade unions, Chartist clubs, factories, Sunday schools, Mechanics' Institutes and book clubs. In Preston were the "Academies" where 18 or 20 men would rent a two-roomed cottage for 1s.9d or 2s. a week, and use the top room for learning to read and write, the bottom room for social meetings.[3] Among long-established town subscription libraries were Lancaster (1768) and Blackburn (1779).[4]

By 1850 there was still no comprehensive national or local scheme for library provision, only a variety of libraries for different social groups and classes. Cities like Manchester and Liverpool enjoyed excellent facilities, towns had reasonable provision but there was little in rural areas.

Sadly, it was just at this time that a notable local library was disappearing. The library in the Parish Church of St. Wilfrid's, Ribchester, was formed in 1684, when "Mr. Hayhurst, Minister of Macclesfield, left all his books (except the Book of Martyrs and his Great Bible) to the Parish Church of Ribchester".[5] The first references to the library in the Churchwardens' Accounts are:[6] "Mr. Hayhurst, Minister of Macclesfield, left all his books (except the Book of Martyrs and his Great Bible) to the Parish Church of Ribchester".[5] The first references to the library in the Churchwardens' Accounts are:[6]

1685. Paid to Mr. Kippax and Henery Hayhurst for ffetching the lyberary given by Mr. Bradley Hayhurst and spent about ye same..	£3 07 04.
1687. Spent when we sett ye work of ye Library..	£0 02 10.
Paid for ye great fflage ffetching, and setting up, and wood belonging to ye same for the Library	..............£0 07 02.
1688. For makeing the hearth in ye Library	.... £0 01 00.
1689. Paid to John Hacking for a table for ye Library	£0 07 00.
Paid for one chaire for ye Library........	£0 01 03.
Paid to Thomas Newsham for mending the leades betwixt ye Church and Lybrary............	£0 01 06.
1691. Item, in placeing the bookes in the Lybrary........	£0 01 06.

By 1856 the President of the Chetham Society, Mr. James Crossley, reported at its Annual Meeting: "He recollected many years ago when he went to Ribchester, that he found there what had been originally a very good patristic and scholastic library, gradually mouldering away, partly from decay, partly from decomposition. On speaking to the clerk on the subject, the reply was, "Why sir, there's nobody here who cares at all about it; and if you would like to have any of the books, you are quite at liberty to take as many as you please". He only took one volume.[7]

Mr. Chancellor Christie in 1885, reported that the Rev. G. W. Reynolds saw the books, in or before 1858, packed in boxes.[8] This was confirmed by the Rev. Boulby Haslewood, son of the late Rector of Ribchester, Rev. B. T. Haslewood, who said, "The books used to be in the chest in the old vestry".[9] In 1889 Tom Smith and the current Rector, Rev. F. J. Dickson, made a search and found 6 volumes, "all in a dilapidated and disgraceful condition", one endorsed "Hayhurst's Library".[10] Do any houses in Ribchester contain books from this lost library?

St. Wilfrid's Church, Ribchester, S.E. View
(The location of a historic (now lost) library)

In the later part of the 19th. century, other institutions had libraries which were not open to the general public. Bushell's Hospital, now a residential home, was founded in a house built by the Rev. William Bushell when he was nominated to the Curacy of Goosnargh in 1692. It opened as a hospital in 1735 for "maintaining, supporting and providing for decayed gentlemen or gentlewomen, or persons of the better rank of

143

both or either sex, inhabitants of the towns or townships of Preston, Euxton, Goosnargh, Whittingham, Fulwood and Elston, being Protestants".[11] In his history of Goosnargh, (described by Tom Smith as "a so-called history; for the style is paltry, the information trite, and the observations generally puerile"),[12] Richard Cookson says, "In the year 1850 the trustees of the Hospital provided a library of about 120 volumes of standard works for the use of the inmates, in which may be found "milk for the weak and meat for the strong". Since 1850 the library has been augmented to 200 volumes".[13]

Schools had to make their own provision for books. At Goosnargh, two schools were served in one building: the Free Grammar School, founded in 1673 by Henry Colbourne, who left money in trust for the use of schools and poor people in the chapelry of Goosnargh, and the Free, or Threlfall School, whose founder, Thomas Threlfall of Whittingham, provided for a school to be set up within a hundred roods of the church or chapel of Goosnargh. The old schoolhouse was pulled down in 1839 and a new building erected. This was enlarged in 1845 at the expense of Richard Oliverson, formerly of Goosnargh. Fishwick records in 1871 that "the school now consists of two rooms on the ground floor, one for girls and one for boys, and a room on the second floor for a library".[14]

Often, schools relied on donations of books. In December 1879 the Preston Pilot reported the "Annual Christmas Tea Meeting of Knowle Green Independent Chapel held in the school room on Thursday...The meeting expressed its gratitude to Mrs. Fenton of Dutton Manor for the generous gift to the library of over 40 volumes".[15] Stonyhurst College already had an outstanding library, with important collections of early printed books, illuminated manuscripts and material on the history of Catholicism in England.[16]

At the time of the Education Act of 1870, something like three-quarters of the population of Britain was without the benefit of a public library service. A substantial addition to the facilities available to the reading public, however, were the libraries and reading rooms maintained by co-operative societies. Although working men had been developing the principles of self-help and co-operation since the early 19th. century, the purpose of the early pioneers was not just to create retail shops, selling wholesome food at fair prices, but to develop social union in a good cause through self-reliance. Whilst co-operation can be defined as an association of shareholders, usually described as members, who as individuals have contributed a fund of capital to be employed under their collective direction for trading purposes, the prime objective was not to secure the largest possible return on capital, but to provide services to members, who were also customers. The members who shopped at the societies and held shares in them, were the same people who formed the committees which made policy decisions, voted on the issues which affected aspects of the society's life and funded educational activities. Co-operation was a total philosophy of self-help and mutual aid, and the role of education in the movement was not a luxury but a basic principle - the advancement of aspirations and ideals.

The Longridge Industrial Co-operative Society was typical of the efforts of groups of working men to establish independent and self-supporting educational systems, including libraries and reading rooms, to increase literacy and to reflect the changing social structure of society. Why was it felt necessary by the working classes to provide sources of reading material for themselves and their fellow workers? Because existing libraries were unavailable to workers because of cost, distance and the middle-class influence and control.

Libraries and reading rooms were a community facility characterised by free provision and availability - channels through which members extended their educational horizons. The libraries held books which instructed members in basic education, in the philosophy of co-operation and the exploration of the wider world through works of fiction. Reading rooms were a place where members met, read about events happening in the world and discussed them, and could consult practical periodicals.

In supporting these ideals from its foundation, the Longridge Co-op. made a grant on the profits from the shops of two and a half per cent per annum to its library, which by 1887 amounted to £40.[17] Use of the Library and Reading Room was free to members and their families. They were administered by the Education Secretary, who also acted as

Librarian. This position was held from 1892 to 1946 by William Helm, of whom it was reported by Ronald Seed, the Acting Education Secretary, that "when unable to attend the Education Committee meeting on Monday, 12 August 1946, it was the first meeting that he had missed since his appointment over 54 years ago".[18]

This photograph taken during the First World War shows Longridge Post Office, then in its current position in Berry Lane and run by A. E. Lewty - Stationer, with alternative reading provision advertised on a poster in the window, "Lending Library. One penny per week". This below "A fresh appeal from Lord Kitchener: another 100,000 men required for the War".

Mr. Helm retired on account of ill-health at the end of 1946 and died the following year. Mr. Seed succeeded him until his own retirement in 1981.

Little is known of the Library's early years, since few records survive of Longridge Co-op. As in too many other cases, there has been a substantial loss of records following mergers of societies.

In 1907 it was reported that "the Society has a good library, consisting of 1,267 volumes, with an average weekly circulation of 120 volumes". The amount granted for all educational purposes was £102.6s.6d. and the Society's membership was 1,133 when Longridge's population was about 4,500.[19]

The 1916 Congress Handbook said that the Longridge Society "has always maintained a well-stocked library of books, from which the villagers, living in an out-of-way place as they do(!!), derive considerable instruction and refined pleasure". There were 1,311 members.[20]

The surviving records of the Longridge Co-op. consist of an incomplete file of quarterly and half-yearly reports and balance sheets, now lodged in the Co-operative Union Library in Holyoake House in Manchester. These cover the period from 1911 to 1955, with gaps. The following information about the Library and Reading Room is taken from the brief reports of the Educational Committee.

The balance sheets of the Educational Fund show a consistently high level of expenditure on books, newspapers and magazines. For example, between 1924 and 1932, total spending on new books was £92.16s.7d. and on newspapers and magazines £138.3s.6d. This was offset by the sale of "old books" which raised £2.7s.4d and of papers and magazines which made £17.2s.5d. Other pieces of information from these files: In future the Library will be open for the loan of books on Saturday afternoons from 2 to 4 o'clock, instead of from 3 to 5 as formerly, this we believe will be more convenient to the readers, (September 1915). With dearer newspapers we note a better attendance. In answer to various inquiries, the Reading Room is open

Free to all Members of the Society, male and female; and though in the past our lady friends have not attended to any great extent, still we see no reason why they should not take advantage of the facilities offered, (June 1917).

Notice of motion received from Mr. John Dodson - that the Reading Room and Library be closed forthwith, owing to the expense entailed. Motion defeated, (June 1923). The Lending Library is open on Friday evening from 7 to 9 p.m., and on Saturday afternoon from 2 to 4 p.m. (September 1926).

Mr. John Dodson moved a Resolution - The Library in connection with the L.I.C.S. Education Dept. be dispensed with - Defeated, (October 1930).

We would also remind you that we are in possession of a Stretcher, this is kept handy behind the Reading Room door, and in these days of road accidents, in case of necessity, the same is available to the public, (March 1931).

In future the Reading Room will be open daily from 6 to 9 p.m., except Saturday, 2 to 8 p.m. We regret that it has been necessary to take this step, but after repeated warnings, and disregarded notices, we had no other option but to close as stated. The Reading Room has had a varied career. Since the Central premises were open over 50 years ago, there has always been a room open daily, at first it was on the front in Berry Lane, now used as a store-room, afterwards for several years in a one-storey building, since demolished, on the ground floor where the Bakery now stands, and can be seen in the picture on the front cover of the Balance Sheet, and since August 17th. 1901 in the room as at present, (December 1932).

After having been closed in the daytime for nearly 12 months, the Reading Room is now open daily from 8.30 a.m. to 9 p.m. and will continue to be for the present, providing the Rooms are used in a satisfactory manner, (September 1933).

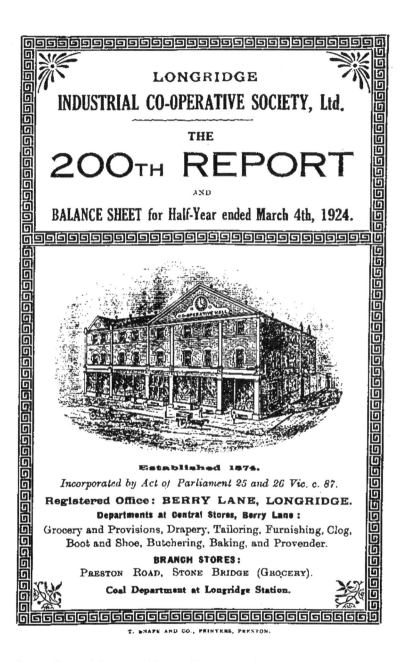

LONGRIDGE
INDUSTRIAL CO-OPERATIVE SOCIETY, Ltd.

THE
200TH REPORT

AND

BALANCE SHEET for Half-Year ended March 4th, 1924.

Established 1874.

Incorporated by Act of Parliament 25 and 26 Vic. c. 87.

Registered Office: BERRY LANE, LONGRIDGE.

Departments at Central Stores, Berry Lane :

Grocery and Provisions, Drapery, Tailoring, Furnishing, Clog,
Boot and Shoe, Butchering, Baking, and Provender.

BRANCH STORES:

PRESTON ROAD, STONE BRIDGE (GROCERY).

Coal Department at Longridge Station.

T. SNAPE AND CO., PRINTERS, PRESTON.

Co-op Central Stores with Reading Room in one storey building on
extreme right.

The Lending Library is now closed, all the books having been returned; as to their disposal, we propose to hold a display and sale in the Lesser Hall on a date yet to be arranged, (June 1935).

Some books, including a set of Cassell's Miniature Library were donated to Balshaws Grammar School, Leyland.[21] A sale of books raised £3.12s.9d.

We very much regret to have to complain of Papers being taken from the table in the Reading Room. This has occurred too frequently lately, and we request the assistance of the members in our endeavour to find out the persons guilty, which we are anxious to do, (March 1937).

After very careful consideration it has been decided to close the Reading Room to the Public from 1st. May 1955. The number of members using it does not justify the expense of keeping it open, (March 1955).

So the Co-operative Society's provision of library and reading facilities ended after 75 years. The Library with shelves on two walls had gone 20 years earlier, and now the familiar Reading Room, with its oak table and armchairs, its newspapers and periodicals, including Co-operative News, Our Circle, Amateur Gardener and Woman's Outlook closed.

The Society had continued to provide a library service to its members alongside the growing public library system. The early part of this article described some local provision for access to books, but our modern public library system dates from 1850.

Before then, almost every political, economic, religious, social and educational group attempted to make some library provision, however inadequate, for its members, but the great and increasing demand for books provided the justification for the Public Libraries Act of 1850.

This was just one, but not the least important, of a series of reforming measures passed in the first half of the 19th. century which led towards a healthier and more democratic society.

It empowered municipal authorities with a population of 10,000 or more to spend a ½d. rate (1d. from 1855) on accommodation for a museum and/or library and for the maintenance of the building, but did not permit expenditure on specimens or books. The Act could only be adopted if a majority of two-thirds of the votes cast in a special poll of ratepayers was secured.

This did not apply to Longridge, which was only created a Board of Health District in 1883 and became an Urban District Council, comprising the townships of Alston and Dilworth, in 1894, when its population was just over 4,000.[22]

In 1919 a further Public Libraries Act abolished the 1d. rate limitation, made possible the extension of the urban library service to meet new and growing needs and gave library powers to counties which facilitated a complementary provision in rural areas. County Councils were constituted as library authorities and henceforth Urban District Councils and parishes could only adopt the Act with the permission of the County Council, though in practice adoption would impose too great a strain on local rates.

In Lancashire, adoption of the 1919 Act was made possible by a grant from the Carnegie United Kingdom Trust of £4,000 to be spent on an initial stock of books and equipment. The County Council's powers for library purposes were delegated to the Education Committee and a Libraries Sub-Committee. The principle adopted for the working of the scheme was the provision of a constant supply of fresh books from a central collection in Preston to local centres established in villages. Centres were to be housed in schools, village institutes or clubs, provided that the books were available to borrowers at definite periods at least once a week, that proper care was taken of them and that appropriate records were kept in good order. The library service was to be entirely free and Urban District and Parish Councils would not incur any financial liability in administering the local service point, though centres had to provide cupboards, shelving, chairs and tables. Detailed guidance was given on the delivery, reception, issue and return of books, a register of borrowers, duties of local librarians, publicity and the notification of infectious diseases. The number of books per centre would initially be between 50 and 500, according to the population at the 1921 Census.[23]

In Longridge and district, centres were opened as follows:

> By 5 October 1925: Grimsargh - The Institute
> By 1 March 1926 : Ribchester - National School.,Thornley - School
>   Whitechapel - School House
> By 21 June 1926 : Chipping - School, Longridge - Council
>   Offices, Market Place[24]

This brief report to the Libraries Sub-Committee is not strictly accurate. The Minutes of Longridge U.D.C. in the 1920s reveal earlier activity and some teething troubles.

15 March 1922 - Ordinary Monthly Meeting. Mr. J. McCreary, Mr. Nicholson and Mr. Waring attended as a deputation to ascertain the Council's view as to the provision of a Public Library and Reading Room. The Clerk explained the Council's difficulty in financing this from the rates and that it would seek assistance from the Carnegie U.K. Trust.[25]

17 May 1922 - Ordinary Monthly Meeting. The Clerk reported that the C.U.K.T. had ceased to entertain applications from Borough and Urban District Councils.[26]

25 May 1925 - Special Meeting. Mr. J. D. Cowley, County Librarian, gave a short address on the working of the scheme. Several places were mentioned as suitable for a centre and the matter was discussed for a considerable period.[27]

21 October 1925 - Ordinary Monthly Meeting. Resolved on the motion of Mr. T. R. Marland, seconded by Mr. J. W. Brown, that the Clerk write to the County Librarian requesting him to send a parcel of books.[28]

30 March 1926 - Ordinary Monthly Meeting. Mr. Marland asked if the time had not arrived when the Council could obtain a Box of Books.

Resolved on the motion of Mr. Marland, seconded by Mr. H. Slater, that the Clerk write to the County Librarian on the matter.[29]

21 July 1926 - Ordinary Monthly Meeting. Mr. Marland enquired if something could be done whereby the Public could have the use of the Books which had been sent by the County Council and were now in boxes in the Council Offices. The Surveyor stated that Mr. Wilding who had promised to act as Honorary Librarian declined to commence his duties unless the books were placed under lock and key. Resolved on the motion of Mr. Marland, seconded by Mr. J. Dodson, that it be left in the hands of the Surveyor to provide a cupboard for the books in the office.[30]

6 September 1926 - Meeting of General Purposes Committee. The Clerk read a letter from the Director of Education dated 4 September 1926 stating that Mr. Wilding had reported to the County Librarian that the centre had not been opened and that he was not satisfied with the arrangements for Housing the Books. The County Librarian suggested that he should visit the Council Offices to discuss the matter. Resolved on the motion of Mr. N. J. Swarbrick, seconded by Mr. W. Houghton, that the Clerk write to the Secretary of the Co-operative Society's Education Committee asking them if they would undertake the Housing and Distribution of the Books.[31]

15 September 1926 - Ordinary Monthly Meeting. The Clerk read a letter from the Secretary of the Longridge Co-operative Society's Education Dept. stating that the Committee were prepared to accept and distribute the Books supplied to the District under the County Library scheme. Resolved on the motion of Mr. J. Edmundson, seconded by Mr. Houghton, that the Clerk write to the Secretary of the Education Committee expressing the Council's thanks and also to the County Librarian informing him of what had been done.[32]

17 November 1926 - Ordinary Monthly Meeting. Mr. Dodson informed the Council that the work of distributing the Books was more than the Librarian could manage and asked if some assistance could be given. Resolved that the Clerk write to Mr. John McCreary and others to ask them to give voluntary assistance.[33]

6 December 1926 - Meeting of General Purposes Committee. The Clerk read a letter from the Secretary of the Education Dept. of Longridge Industrial Co-op. Soc. stating that the work in connection with The Library Scheme entailed too much work, that the Committee were not prepared to continue same and that they intended to return same. Resolved on the motion of Mr. Slater, seconded by Mr. Swarbrick that the Clerk write to the Education Committee asking them to allow the books to remain until voluntary help was obtained and to arrange for the Books to be distributed on the nights when the Books belonging to the Society's Library were not issued.[34]

Berry Lane has seen almost all locations for the County Library Service
Co-op building and R. Smith's C.E. School on right, current
Branch Library behind trees top left.

15 December 1926 - Ordinary Monthly Meeting. The Clerk read a letter from Mr. J. McCreary in which he stated that he had had an interview with the Co-operative Society's Librarian and had volunteered to give assistance but that he had found that it was not assistance he required but remuneration and that his services were not required. Mr. McCreary stated that he would willingly give assistance if the Council decided on any other method of distribution. Mr. McCreary was thanked for his kindness.[35]

By 4 November 1929, the Longridge centre had moved from the Co-operative Society to R. Smith's Boys C. E. School, where pupils including Ron Seed and Ivy Leeming helped the teachers to issue the books on one evening per week. The only record in the School Log Book is from 28 May 1930, "Received a fresh consignment of County Library books".[36]

Other new centres were:
By 2 December 1929: Bleasdale - School.
By 2 November 1931: Knowle Green - Institute.
By 7 November 1932 : Goosnargh - School.[37]

Whilst new centres were being opened, provision was also being made for less fortunate users. As early as March 1928 it had been recorded that "worn-out books should be presented to Mental Hospitals", and cleaner books were sent to the Whittingham Asylum. New books were later supplied to patients not on "destructive" wards, and for the staff.[38]

In the 1930s, the County Library recognised that the existing mode of provision was under strain. There was a need for full-time or part-time branch libraries that were purpose-built, and for salaried librarians instead of voluntary helpers. It was difficult to afford an adequate supply of books and there were no funds for newspapers and periodicals.

In September 1936, while library services were still provided from the Boys' School, tenders were received for the supply of a roller shutter bookcase fitting, and the tender of £34 from J. Cartmell and Sons of Preston was accepted.[39]

By the following year, Longridge was identified by the County Librarian as one of the 13 towns and villages where small new or adapted buildings were likely to be required for a branch library, and it was formally included in the building programme.[41] In May 1938 the Clerk to Longridge U.D.C. made a formal request to the County Council for the provision of a library in the village, since the existing facilities in the Boys' School would no longer be available.[42]

In September 1938, the Libraries Sub-Committee received a report on the lease of premises for a proposed branch library at Longridge. This pointed out that the population was about 4,000 and served only by a library centre, open for one evening each week, since 1926. The total issues for 1937-38 were 16,932. It was agreed to take a three year lease, with an option to renew for a period of three years, on two shops in Market Place, belonging to Mr. Sanderson, who would be prepared to carry out structural alterations to meet the County Council's requirements.

County Branch Library, Market Place, centre, leased from Sanderson, Butcher, left 1938-1964

The accommodation would then comprise a Lending Dept., 40ft. by 20ft., Store Room and lavatory, and the rent charged would be 15s. per week, exclusive of rates. The lease was agreed, as from 1 December 1938.[42]

The following March tenders were accepted for interior fittings[43]

   a) Providing and laying "A" super quality linoleum:
      Messrs. Parkinsons (Preston) Ltd.   £36 - 0 - 0
   b) Providing and fixing fittings, gas fires, water heaters etc:
      Mr. A. G. Nichols, Longridge.   £112 - 2 - 6

The Longridge Branch Library opened in June 1939, with part-time provision on three days a week. For administrative purposes it was linked with the new Kirkham Branch, under a Branch Librarian, with a junior assistant, who both divided their time between the two service points. The neighbouring centres of Chipping, Grimsargh, Knowle Green, Ribchester and Thornley were connected to Longridge for the purpose of exchanging their book stocks.[44]

The first Branch Librarian, transferred from Kearsley, was Miss E. Wild (1939 - 1942), followed by Miss Freda L. Shaw, later Mrs. Lewis (1942 - 1944), Miss D. N. Rosser (1944 - 1946) and Miss B. A. Staddon (1947 - 1951). Early junior assistants were Miss E. M. Houghton (1939 -1941), Miss P. M. Saunders (1941), Miss M. Rawcliffe, later Mrs. Broadbent (1941 - 1946), Miss E. J. Proud (1946), Miss I. Dagger (1946), Mr. R. Ashworth (1946 - 1947) and Miss L. Robinson who from 1947 represented Longridge Library for a generation of users.[45]

The lease on the Market Place premises continued to be renewed at three yearly intervals, although when it was found to be badly affected by damp in 1943, other accommodation was sought. It was not possible to find an alternative location so remedial work was carried out, involving the provision of ventilators and three additional gas radiators at a total cost of £70.15s.8d.[46]

In 1954 the County Library drew up a new building programme. According to the policy criteria, Longridge was identified as deserving a full-time branch library on a ¼ to ½ acre site. The surrounding communities -- Aighton, Bailey and Chaigley, Chipping, Goosnargh, Ribchester and Whittingham - were described as having populations so scattered that they were better served by mobile libraries. However, it was to be 26 February 1964 before the new Longridge Library, in the grounds of The Limes in Berry Lane was opened by His Honour Judge P. Ingress Bell T.D., Q.C.

Longridge now has a modern and busy branch library, part of a county system moving beyond the traditional supply of books, through the more recent records, videos and CDs, and into areas of lifelong learning and services in information technology. At a time when local library users can learn about the Internet, it is worth recalling that until 1965 there was no compulsion on any local authority to make library provision. Before then provision was essentially a voluntary activity, requiring in its early phases the specific consent of the ratepayers. The public library service was one of the most important social and cultural developments of the 19th. and 20th. centuries, and free universal access to books only became available in Longridge and district in living memory.

NOTES

1. KELLY, T. Public libraries in Great Britain before 1850. 1966. p. 33.
2. DAVIS, S. W. The history of Lancashire County Library. 1967. p. 24.
3. CROSBY, A. A history of Lancashire. 1998. p. 113
4. HAMMOND, J. L. and B. The age of the Chartists. 1930. p. 330. n. 3 (quoting the Preston Temperance Advocate, June 1837).
5. GASKELL, Bishop F. Notitia Cestriensis. Chetham Society Publications. O.S. Vol. XXII. 1850. p. 471.
6. SMITH, T. C. and SHORTT, Rev. J. The history of the Parish of Ribchester in the   County of Lancaster. 1890. p. 214.
7. Ibid. p. 215.
8. CHRISTIE, R. C. The old church and school libraries of Lancashire. Chetham Society Publications. N.S. Vol. VII. 1885. p. 104.
9. SMITH, T. C. and SHORTT, Rev. J. op. cit. pp. 215-216.
10. Ibid. p. 216.
11. FISHWICK, H. A history of the parochial chapelry of Goosnargh in the County of Lancaster. 1871. p. 127.
12. SMITH, T. C. A history of Longridge and district. 1888. p. 244.
13. COOKSON, R. Goosnargh : past and present. 1888. p. 217.
14. FISHWICK, H. op. cit. pp. 128-130.
15. Preston Pilot, 31 December 1879, p. 4.
16. NODAL, J. H. In Transactions of the Library Association. 1879. p.141
17. SMITH, T. C. op. cit. p. 89.
18. Longridge Industrial Co-operative Society. 290th. Report and Balance Sheet for half-year ended 5 September 1946. p. 18.
19. Preston : a Handbook to the 39th. Annual Co-operative Congress. Whitsuntide, 1907. Compiled by the Handbook Committee. 1907. p.130.
20. Lancaster : a Souvenir of the 48th. Co-operative Congress. Whitsuntide, 1916. Compiled by the Handbook Committee. 1916. p.170.
21. Information from Mr. R. Seed.
22. TILL, J. M. A history of Longridge and its people. 1993. pp. 36, 118.
23. LANCASHIRE RECORD OFFICE. ELM/1. pp. 3-5.

24. L. R. O. ELM/1. pp. 16, 25, 27.
25. L. R. O. UDLo 1/14. p. 156.
26. L. R. O. UDLo 1/14. p. 174.
27. L. R. O. UDLo 1/15. p. 178.
28. L. R. O. UDLo 1/15. p. 212.
29. L. R. O. UDLo 1/15. p. 251.
30. L. R. O. UDLo 1/16. p. 41.
31. L. R. O. UDLo 1/16. p. 50.
32. L. R. O. UDLo 1/16. p. 52.
33. L. R. O. UDLo 1/16. p. 74.
34. L. R. O. UDLo 1/16. p. 80.
35. L. R. O. UDLo 1/16. p. 83.
36. L. R. O. SMLn 1/2. p. 419.
37. L. R. O. ELM/1. pp. 80, 93, 129, 158.
38. DAVIS, S. W. op. cit. p. 249.
39. L. R. O. ELM/2. p. 17.
40. L. R. O. ELM/2. p. 65.
41. L. R. O. UDLo 1/20. p. 197.
42. L. R. O. ELM/2. p. 87.
43. L. R. O. ELM/2. p. 111.
44. L. R. O. ELM/2. p. 113.
45. L. R. O. ELM/2. pp. 128, 135, 183, 190. ELM/3. pp. 13, 64, 135, 141, 162, 164, 166.

LIST OF SUBSCRIBERS

Mr & Mrs G.E. Airey, Thornley
Bruce & Christine Alder, Longridge
Brian & Caroline Alston, Clitheroe
Mr Harry Alston, Longridge
Mr W. Atkinson, Longridge
Rev Richard Awre, Vicar of Longridge
   (1989-1999), Warwickshire
Alston Lane Catholic Primary School,
   Alston
Mr J. & Mrs M.E. Ashton, Longridge
Mr Robert Bailey, Clitheroe
Mr & Mrs B.D. Bamber, Longridge
Mrs M. Bamber, Garstang
Thomas Banks & Co (Coal Merchant),
   Preston
Mr J. Barrow, Preston
Mr & Mrs J. Birkett, Longridge
Mrs Jo Blackwell, Longridge
Mrs D. Bradley, Longridge
Mr R. Brewer, Longridge
Mrs Sheila Bridge, Grimsargh
Colin & Sheila Brierley, Longridge
Syd Brown & Sons Ltd, Longridge
Mrs Mavis Byrne, Ribchester
Mr & Mrs C.M.J. Carefoot, Chatburn
Mr & Mrs Charles D. Carefoot,
   Fulwood
Mr & Mrs R. Geoff Carefoot,
   Longridge
Mr W. & Mrs E. Carefoot, Longridge
Dr & Mrs W. Clive Carefoot, Chipping
Mrs M. Cartwright, Hurst Green
Chipping Local History Society
Christchurch (Methodist/URC),
   Longridge
Miss D. F. Clay, Longridge
Councillor Pam Cliff, Longridge Town
   Mayor   1999-2000

Mr Harold Collinson, Fulwood
Mr W. & Mrs R. Cookson, Longridge
Mr & Mrs S. Cookson, Chipping
John & Rae Cotterall, Southport
Mrs K. Coupe, Longridge
Maureen Cousin (Ladies Fashions),
   Longridge
Mr M. Croasdale, Longridge
Brenda & Peter Croft, Grimsargh
Dr Alan Crosby, Preston
Mr Frank & the late Mrs Margaret Day,
   Longridge
Mr & Mrs David Dickinson, Chipping
Bob Dobson, Staining
Mr A.R. Dodd, Goosnargh
P.T. Doherty (Joiner), Longridge
Mr & Mrs J.C. Donnelly, Longridge
Mrs Jean Downham, Longridge
Mr & Mrs Harry Eagles, Longridge
Mr & Mrs Nigel Earnshaw, Berkshire
Mr & Mrs Paul Earnshaw, Kent
Mrs E. Edmondson, Longridge
Mr & Mrs P.J. English, Alston
Mr John Farmery (Longridge Pet Store)
Mrs Jacinth Fitch, Thornley
Mrs S. Fogg, Fulwood
Herbert T. Forrest Ltd (Building
   Contractors), Longridge
Dr Ian Forrester, Longridge
Rev Peter Furness, Longridge
Mr James Gardner, Longridge
Mrs Susan Gaunt, Longridge
Ann Goulding, Longridge
Mr K.W. & Mrs E.Y. Gornall,
   Longridge
Louis A. Gornall. Cabus
Mr & Mrs George Gray, Montreal,
   Canada

Ms Christine A. Green, Longridge
Mr A. Heap, Longridge
Mr Tom Heginbotham, Grimsargh
Mr Derek Hicks, Longridge
Mrs Doreen Hoggarth, Grimsargh
Andrew & Trisha Holden, Longridge
D.E. Holden & Co, Longridge
Miss Gertrude Holden, Longridge
HSBC Bank plc, Longridge
Olive Hurlstone, Longridge
Wilf Ireland, Longridge
Marian Isherwood, Goosnargh
Walter Jackson, Ribbleton
Mr & Mrs Tony James, Ribchester
Miss Heather M. Jenkinson, Blackburn
Jones Stroud Insulations, Longridge
Marjorie Kellett, Longridge
Mr & Mrs T. Kennedy
    (Durham Ox), Longridge
Norman Kenyon, Longridge
Mrs June Kiernon, Hothersall
Mr T.H. Laker, Longridge
Mr A. Lamper, Ribchester
Lancashire County Library Service,
    Preston
Mrs J. Langley, Longridge
Mr D.J. Lavis, Ribchester
Mrs Lucy Lawer, Cornwall
Mrs Elaine Leech, Longridge
Mrs Nora Leece, Longridge
Mr Richard Leighton, Longridge
The Limes Pre-School Nursery,
    Longridge
Mr & Mrs F. Little, Longridge
Mrs Joan Littler, Blackburn
Longridge Branch Library
Longridge C.E. Primary School
Longridge Conservative Club
Longridge County High School
Longridge G.M. Primary School
Longridge Sports & Leisure

Longridge Teaching Centre
Longridge Town Council
Mr J. & Mrs K. Longworth, Grimsargh
Mr & Mrs W.R. Marsden, Stonyhurst
Mrs Valerie Martin-Warren, Longridge
Mrs P.C. Mayne (Kids in Mind),
    Longridge
Mr & Mrs D.G. McNamara, Grimsargh
Mr G. & Mrs M. Melling, Longridge
Mr J. Melling, MBE & Mrs R. Melling,
    Longton
Susan Metcalf, Longridge
Peter H. Morgan MBE, Dutton
National Westminster Bank plc,
    Longridge
Bernard & Joan Nichols, Claughton-on-
    Brock
Mr William Norcross, Preston
North West Sound Archive, Clitheroe
Nu Bodyz Fitness Centre, Longridge
Mrs Jackie Nuttall, Bedfordshire
Tom Nuttall, Grimsargh
Mr A.W. Panter, Longridge
Mr William Park, Preston
Mr Norman Parker, Longridge
Mr Jim Parkinson, Longridge
David & Pauline Paterson, Chipping
Mr Terence Pattinson, Longridge
Dr Kevin Pavey, Longridge
Margaret & Eddie Paynter, Longridge
Elizabeth & Mike Pearson, Hothersall
Mr Harry Pinder, Ribchester
Mrs Norah Pinder, Longridge
Mrs Frances Prince, Whalley
Mrs Jean Procter, Knowle Green
Mrs Josephine Procter, Longridge
Miss Alison Reese, Longridge
Councillor J.S. Reese, Longridge
Mr Brian Rhodes, Longridge
Ribble Farm Fare (Wholesale
    Greengrocers), Longridge

Ribble Valley Tourism, Clitheroe
Ribchester Museum Trust
Mrs J. Rich, Longridge
Mrs Margaret Roberts, Longridge
Carole & Joe Robinson, Longridge
Mrs E. Roughley (Towneley Arms), Longridge
Royal British Legion (Longridge Branch)
St Lawrence & St Paul Parish, Longridge
St Wilfrid's R.C. Church, Longridge
St Wilfrid's R.C. Primary School, Longridge
Mr & Mrs F. Salthouse, Longridge
Mr John Scott, Longridge
Bernard & Gillian Seed, Longridge
Mrs Jean Seed, Longridge
Mr John Simpson, Goosnargh
Mr D. Skilbeck, Longridge
Fred Slater, Longridge
Mr John Slater, Longridge
Mr Martin B. Slater, Longridge
Dr John B. Smethurst, Eccles
Councillor David Smith, Longridge
Mr G. & Mrs M. Smith, Longridge
Mrs Melene Spencer, Longridge
Peter Spinks (TV & VCR), Longridge
Spout Farm Nursery, Longridge
Mrs Peggy Parker Starkie, Darwen

Mrs Margaret Swarbrick, Longridge
Mr R.N. & Mrs D. Swarbrick, Longridge
A. Swift & Son Ltd, Longridge
Syngyn Interior Design, Longridge
Martin & Lola Taylor, Longridge
Stephen Taylor (Opticians), Longridge
Mr W.G. Taylor, Longridge
Sqdn Leader & Mrs M. Tetlow, Buckinghamshire
Rev Peter & Mrs Sylvia Thomas, Longridge
Mr & Mrs John Till, Bleasdale
Mrs Jean Tomlinson, Thornley
Mr Albert Wake, Longridge
Barry & Gillian Walker, Longridge
Peggy Walker, Longridge
James R. Wallbank, Longridge
Mr & Mrs G.D. Walley, Longridge
Mr R. & Mrs S. Walmsley, Longridge
Mr & Mrs B.S. Walton, Longridge
Mr J. & Mrs J. Warburton, Longridge
Mrs Eileen Watson, Lostock Hall
Wilcock Insurance Group, Longridge
Mavis Wilkinson, Longridge
Mr & Mrs K.G. Willan, Longridge
Mrs Sheila Woodburn, Longridge
Working Class Movement Library, Salford